D1341719

no man an island

WRITTEN WITH great insight, this unusual and revealing biography
describes how, as a war-time pilot, Peter Spencer lost the use of
both arms in a cruelly ironic accident. It tells how he pulled himself back from death after it was predicted he would not survive;
how he fought to rebuild his life and prove that a man considered
finished as a human being could ultimately achieve fulfilment and,
through it all, preserve his sense of humour.

Over the years Peter taught himself innumerable skills, and became
a painter of note, husband of the exuberant June Lynette, singer and
actress, father of two delightful children; a town-councillor, public
speaker (including several television appearances), traveller
throughout the world, and ambassador for the International
Association of Mouth and Foot Painting Artists. Having largely
overcome his own disabilities he now devotes a considerable amount
of his time to helping others!

It is a story which will leave the reader almost breathless with
admiration for the unquenchable spirit of optimism, hope and
dogged determination which resulted in the triumph of the human
spirit over almost impossible odds.

The Geranium was Peter's first painting to be accepted by Association of Mouth & Foot Painting Artists.

no man an island

a biography of Peter Spencer
by Eileen Waugh

foreword by

Douglas Bader C.B.E. D.S.O. D.F.C.

a Triton book

This book is dedicated to
Bruce Waugh
in the hope that he will
enjoy reading it.

SBN: 363 00025 9

Distributed by British Printing Corporation Ltd.
St. Giles House, Poland Street, London W.1
Made and printed in Great Britain by
The Garden City Press Limited
Letchworth, Hertfordshire

Acknowledgements

I would like to thank all those who willingly gave up their time or helped by searching their records for necessary data in connection with this book, in particular Squadron Leader W. F. Danton, Air Marshal Sir John Whitley, the staff of the Chessington R.A.F. Rehabilitation Unit, the Ministry of Defence, Sir Herbert Seddon, Mr. Arthur Orr, and finally Madge Fenn for her perceptive insight and generous encouragement.

Illustrations

Author's Note

I FIRST met Peter Spencer when I was doing the research for an article on the Mouth and Foot Painting Artists' Association. His personality made an instant impact on me. Although he was disabled, he looked happy – with laughter lines around his eyes, a friendly smile, and a kindly sense of humour. There was no sign of bitterness, which etches its revealing lines in a face and ultimately destroys. I felt no pity, only admiration as I talked to him.

What was the secret? I wanted to find out how this man, who had been deprived of so much of what most of us consider essential, had learnt to live in harmony with life and, instead of retreating into himself and letting others wait on him, had gone out into the world to lead an active, creative, and wholly satisfying existence.

Because he is a modest man not given to talking about himself or others in depth, and because there were many gaps in his memory, the task was not an easy one although it was extremely worthwhile. I had innumerable interviews with all the members of his family, with his associates, friends, teachers, relations, and anyone who had had any lasting contact with him. I wrote hundreds of letters, we met and corresponded regularly and at length, by tape and letter. I lived in his home with his family, who accepted me with complete naturalness. I read letters, reference books, press cuttings and scrapbooks.

The result is a story, not of sorrow but of happiness and achievement made in the face of great odds, by a man who loves and is loved by many people: his wife and children, his parents and friends. He has learnt not only to extract a great deal from life, but to give his utmost to it.

Bursledon, 1970   EILEEN WAUGH

Foreword

THIS BIOGRAPHY of Peter Spencer is fascinating. I read it straight through without putting it down. The author writes with delicacy, understanding and descriptive technique which is essential for this type of story. Her subject is a young man, keen to fly and fight for his country in the Hitler war. Her description of his initial flying training in Florida, U.S.A., in the summer of 1943, his return to England early in 1944 and subsequent operational training, will ring a nostalgic bell for many of Peter Spencer's generation.

Eileen Waugh is at her best, however, in her revealing and accurate interpretation of Peter Spencer's state of mind as he lay in a hospital bed, minus his right arm, his neck fractured, his left arm paralysed, and in continuing pain. He was twenty years old; the date March 1945. His conscious thoughts ranged from suicidal despair to obstinate determination to live. The writer's insight is penetratingly true.

This is a great story about a man who resolutely accepted Fate's challenge and decided to go on living a normal life. His long and inarticulate courtship of the attractive and talented June Lynette who became his wife is one of the best parts of the book. The reader is left with the impression that without June's wonderful character Peter would not have achieved the seemingly impossible, and there would have been no story to write.

London, 1970   DOUGLAS BADER

> "*No man is an island, entire of itself;*
> *any man's death diminishes me,*
> *because I am involved in mankind.*"

JOHN DONNE

Chapter One

On MARCH 27th, 1943, Peter Nelson Spencer joined the R.A.F. with a high heart to help fight the war in the air.

On March 27th, 1945, six weeks before the end of that war, he lay in a hospital bed in the South of England with his neck broken, his right arm amputated at the shoulder, and his left arm paralysed. He was just twenty years old.

Until that moment, life for Peter had been pretty wonderful – despite the war, despite everything. He was a calm, cheerful, handsome youth, with a buoyancy of spirit which glided over the few problems he had encountered so far, as though unaware of their existence.

Born on August 20th, 1924, in Wallasey, Cheshire, just across the river Mersey from Liverpool, he was still at Oldershaw Grammar School when war was declared, but as soon as the Air Training Corps was formed in Wallasey, Peter joined 273 Squadron. Always keen, he was the first cadet to become a Flight Sergeant and as soon as he was old enough he applied for a University Air Training Corps Scholarship.

When he went for his interview in Padgate, Cheshire, the R.A.F. Recruiting Officer eyed him thoughtfully.

"Why do you want to be a pilot?"

"I want to have a crack at the Hun, sir."

"And what sort of pilot do you want to be?"

"A night fighter pilot."

"Why? Can you see particularly well in the dark?"

"Well, I've been eating a lot of carrots lately, sir," said Peter with a grin.

The Officer roared with laughter, and Peter was convinced that this small incident helped him to get in. Although his excellent school record and the fact that he was classed as "exceptional" by his Commanding Officer in the A.T.C. might also have had something to do with it!

Peter had six interesting and absorbing months at Pembroke College, Cambridge. He enjoyed rowing, played scrum half for the College XV, and joined fully in the social life, as well as concentrating on meteorology, navigation, and subjects likely to be useful to him in the R.A.F. Then followed a Grading School to assess whether he had the ability to become a pilot, and in July 1943 he left the port of Liverpool bound for the U.S.A., travelling via Moncton, Canada, to the No. 5 British Flying Training School in Clewiston, Florida.

Arriving in Florida with its golden sunshine by day and fantasia of lights by night, was like stepping on to the shores of paradise after the blackouts of England and the sardine-packed trip across the Atlantic in the unescorted transport ship, *Pasteur*.

Clewiston was ninety miles from Miami and seventy from Palm Beach, the millionaires' playground. It was a land of abundance, of palm trees and citrus groves, mosquitoes and tropical storms, blistering heat and miles of white sands, but above all: friendliness.

The Americans took the R.A.F. cadets to their hearts. Nothing was too good for them; it was open house all the way; parties and girls, swimming, dancing – and music. Peter's natural charm made him welcome wherever he went.

"C'm on Pete, how about a tune," they would say, pushing him towards the piano, and he was only too happy to oblige, for he had been playing the piano since the age of seven. He liked to play to himself, and he liked to play to others and have them gather round and sing. Anything – from classical music to the hit tune of the moment – and anywhere: in people's homes, in the mess, or at the Clewiston Inn. They even carted the piano on to the grass at the airfield and he played stripped to the waist, his taut young body tanned by the sun.

Fond of all sport and like a fish in the water, Peter spent much of his free time in the pool at Clewiston, glorying in the physical exhilaration of diving in and feeling his body slice through the water. After sitting inactive for several hours being taught the theory of flying, it felt doubly good to be in action again.

On most mornings Peter was up at five-thirty and in the air before seven, marching out to the flight line before dawn – and what a glorious dawn it was: the sky streaked with crimson and gold, the air untouched and fragrant before the day's heat descended. Then cranking up the inertia starter and taking off for a cross country flight over the swamps and citrus groves, dodging round the local thunderstorms, learning to snap roll and slow roll and fly on instruments only.

It was a thrilling, never to be forgotten time of comradeship, high spirits and fun, a series of golden days snatched from the edge of war. Flying itself was a wonderful sensation and Peter never got over the joy of it.

He soon found himself acquiring Americanisms. One night on a cross country flight over mid-Florida, his American instructor asked,

"Where is that, Mr. Spencer?"

"I guess that's the town of Sebring," Peter said.

"When you are in the air you don't *guess*, Mr. Spencer. You gotta *know* where you are."

At weekends he and his friends, Peter Pullan, Monty Manners and Peter Orchard would hitchhike into Palm Beach. Sometimes a large flashy car would pull up and half a dozen negroes moved over to make room for them.

"Very proud to have you Britishers with us," they'd say.

"I'se gonna fight for Uncle Sam next week," one told Peter with a proud grin.

One of the many attractions of Palm Beach was Mrs. Ira Nesmith, a second "Mom" to them all. She was a Canadian whose favourite nephew had been killed in the Canadian Air Force and, by befriending sixty to a hundred British cadets every week, she and her husband made a very real contribution to the war effort. Some of them stayed with her, some with her friends, and some in a dormitory of thirty beds specially prepared for them. Wherever they were, these "British boys so far from home" were made to feel welcome. Throughout the war years she gave hospitality to over fifteen hundred boys, and in 1947 she was awarded His Majesty's Medal for Service in the Cause of Freedom.

"Owing to a shortage of metal in the United Kingdom," wrote the British Embassy, "some time will elapse before the insignia of your decoration can be sent, but arrangements are being made for a ribbon to be presented to you in the near future..."

The United Kingdom eventually overcame this slight difficulty, and the medal was presented to Mrs. Nesmith on a British warship just off the coast of Florida.

During his six months stay at Clewiston, Peter wrote to his local paper in Wallasey:

"We are training over here with several American aviation cadets who are a grand lot and, apart from occasional friendly arguments about the qualifications of the Spitfire and the Thunderbolt, we get on very well together. This is, perhaps, one of the best ways of promoting Anglo-American friendship."

This sentiment was echoed by an American cadet who wrote in the airfield's *Fly Paper* magazine, "Listening Out Course 16", which was edited by Monty Manners with Peter on the staff:

"We have had some pretty heated debates at times, but that is what has made our stay here the more perfect. The fact that we have lived together for six months and have never failed to respect each other's opinions has proven to all of us that the Great Britain-United States alliance is constructed on a truly solid foundation ... Now, as I leave Florida, I feel a sense of loss at leaving all the British friends I have made here ..."

There were three Pilot's Courses in operation simultaneously at Clewiston. Course No. 15 was still there when the new cadets had arrived. They were told,

"On every course there have always been at least two cadets killed."

Peter and his colleagues eyed each other speculatively. Was it possible that before the six months were out two of them would be dead? On which two would fate pounce? Then, being young and optimistic, with the ability to live in the present and let tomorrow take care of itself, Peter promptly banished the thought.

But one night, on a long cross country flight, fog sprang up suddenly and eclipsed the Riddle Airfield where they normally landed. Most of the cadets were diverted to Clewiston Airport, including Peter and his navigator, Peter Pullan. They had a particularly tricky landing to negotiate as the flare path had been laid across a narrow gap between two deep ditches, and the moment Peter had landed them safely without damage to either themselves or the aircraft, they both climbed out overjoyed and, going down on their hands and knees, symbolically kissed the earth.

But it was on this trip that the prophesy came true.

15

Two cadets never returned. They had crashed when trying to land using a beam approach system near Fort Myers.

Peter flew solo for the first time three days after his nineteenth birthday. It was a marvellous feeling being up there on his own, soaring through the sky, 1,000 feet above the earth. If anything went wrong there was no one to rely on now – only himself – and there was something satisfying about that thought. It was even more satisfying when, after taking the Stearman P.T. 17 round the circuit and landing the prescribed three times, Peter finally returned to the flight line, switched off the engine and climbed out of the cockpit to receive the congratulations of his instructor and his friends.

Asssessed as an "above average pilot", Peter received his Wings in February 1944, presented by his Commanding Officer, R.A.F. Wing Commander A. A. de Gruyther. It was a proud moment – the culmination of all he had been working for and, although he was sorry to leave, he was also anxious to get home and on to an operational squadron.

Peter arrived back in Wallasey in April, and his parents just had time to greet their only son with open arms when he was off once more to learn to fly all over again from airfields dotted across England, where the conditions were so different from the untrammelled countryside of Florida.

At Sealand, nineteen miles from home, he renewed his acquaintance with Tiger Moths. He had first flown these aircraft at the Grading School in Cambridge. They were old-fashioned bi-planes with an open cockpit, but an interesting aircraft to fly and lots of fun. Next he took a conversion course on twin-engined Oxfords, having only learnt to fly single-engined aircraft in the States. Then followed Calverley, Wrexham, N. Wales, and a short spell at the B.A.T. Flight, Cranage, learning to fly aircraft at night and landing on instruments only.

Finally he went to an Operational Training Unit in Leicester East to fly Dakotas, a companionable aircraft, a little slow but safe, and Peter always felt at home inside them. On September 23rd, 1944, he joined 512 Squadron of 46 Group Transport Command at Broadwell, Oxfordshire.

Peter soon recovered from his disappointment at not becoming a fighter pilot, for he was, after all, doing a highly useful and dangerous job. As the official R.A.F. report on Transport Command says:

"No more highly trained body of men has ever gone out to war. The pilots of Transport Command were phlegmatic and imperturbable. Nature in friendly and fierce mood had no power to daunt them."

From September 1944 to that fateful day on March 27th, 1945, Peter was part of a close-knit crew of four, whose average age was no more than nineteen. George Smith, the pilot, was dark, well-built and a non-smoker. The only married one of the four, he was a hearty, convivial, mercurial type, who enjoyed going out dancing or having a drink with the boys.

Ken Thwaites, the navigator, was tall and affable with a thin neck and curly hair. He had a sense of humour, and enjoyed doing slightly mad things, like being absent without leave or driving to Oxford without a licence.

Bert Dolman, the wireless operator, was a little chap, very good natured, with a thin face and dark greasy hair. He talked to anyone, smoked incessantly and was very fond of his bed. Ken was always ribbing him about it.

Peter was the co-pilot and, according to Ken, their "stabilising influence". Very good looking, with black curly hair, deep set grey eyes, a direct gaze and a warm and friendly smile, he was calm, self possessed and reliable. You could never imagine him giving way to panic or losing his control. He was no rebel, but accepted and enjoyed life as it was.

These four went everywhere together. They were normally up at five in the morning with a take off due at six. Smithy, Peter and Ken dashed off for the briefing usually fully dressed but there were occasions when Peter just had time to pull his uniform on over his pyjamas while Bert still lay fast asleep in bed. Regularly they climbed in the aircraft, warmed it up, did the usual checks, and were just about to take off when Bert would rush up and fall breathless into his seat behind the pilot.

Their job was to support the troops following the invasion of France, taking supplies as near as they could to the front line, and landing on airstrips which were often simply made from wire mesh laid across open fields. They also practised dropping paratroopers and towing and dropping gliders. When towing these gliders at 2,000 feet they were literally sitting ducks waiting to be shot at, for they were only able to fly at a mere 150 m.p.h.

If it was a favourable day they might climb up to 3,000 feet, cross over the coast at Eastbourne and land in Belgium, France or Holland with a load of goods and equipment which could include anything from ammunition to toilet rolls, the cases sometimes packed so tight they had to crawl over the top to get to the cockpit.

They were met by lorries who took off all the supplies, and then the ambulances arrived with wounded to be taken back to England. These men came straight from the battle grounds with only an emergency dressing. There were some terrible sights: men without legs, or arms, and Peter used to wonder what life held for them. One man had had the top of his head blown off; he was only just alive, the bandage stained dark red, and the pulse in his head throbbing. They immediately radioed back to make sure there was a doctor and ambulance waiting at the

18

other end for the emergency cases, as every minute counted.

The next day they were told there was an ENSA party to take back, which offered a spot of light relief, and they were quite bucked, visualising a crowd of pretty girls. It was a considerable anti-climax when the R.A.F. Gang Show turned up, with Douglas Cardew Robinson as the most glamorous thing amongst them.

Frequently they had two runs to Europe and back in a day, but once the day's work was over they had a meal and got spruced up, and if it was a Saturday night they went into Witney for a dance or down to Burford to one of the pubs where they had a few drinks and spent a convivial evening together.

Peter almost invariably spent his leaves in Wallasey. He both liked and admired his parents and they were always delighted to see their only son. A kindly, church-going, good-living couple, they had lived in Wallasey and Liverpool all their lives.

Nelson Spencer was a man small in stature but not in spirit. Born in 1896, his parents had been poor but he was brought up in a stable atmosphere of security and affection until his father died suddenly when Nelson was eight years old. Wiry and active, with a mop of dark curly hair, he then became a boarder at the famous Liverpool Blue-coat "Hospital", a charity school supported by the Liverpool gentry.

Here, Nelson led a rigorous, monastic life of strict discipline, plain food and high principles. Apart from their annual fortnight's holiday, the only occasion on which he and his brother were permitted to see – but not to speak to – their mother was at chapel service on Sundays. A code of honour ran throughout the school and great emphasis was laid on spiritual and moral teaching. Nelson came through the experience idealistic, unassuming and diligent, with a puckish sense of fun and an inborn integrity. He had not forgotten his parents' dictum that to give and receive love is the basis of happiness – but that love must be shared.

At the age of fifteen, Nelson was taken on as office boy in a Liverpool firm of Railway Wagon Builders, and in 1915 he enlisted in the newly formed Bantam Battalion of the Cheshire Regiment. Two days later, to his surprise and pleasure, he received a letter wishing him good luck as a soldier from the G.P.O. telephone operator whose voice had so delighted him whenever he had answered the firm's telephone switchboard.

In March 1916 he met Beatrice Ingle for the first time. It was love at first sight. Spring was in the air and that weekend leave for Nelson was the happiest he had ever spent. He took Beatrice to see "Tulip Time" at the Empire Theatre, Liverpool. They had to stand at the back because the house was full, but this was no hardship. Nelson held Beatrice's hand and, looking down into her eyes the colour of gentians, thought how beautiful she was and how fortune had blessed him. Thus began a memorable and enchanting courtship.

Not long after, Nelson was sent to join the British troops in Belgium. He lived in the trenches under constant bombardment, in mud and filth, with rats and lice for companions. Inches from death every day, he watched men die beside him. Beatrice's letters kept him sane. He was convinced that the inch-high golliwog – a charm she sent for his protection and which never left his side – kept death at bay. Without her, he did not believe he would have survived.

In August 1918 he was awarded the Military Medal for bravery, for rescuing the wounded and dressing their wounds under enemy machine gun fire, and on October 12th Nelson himself was wounded and sent back to England.

Once out of hospital, Nelson returned to his old job –

and to Beatrice. They were married at Easter, on April 18th, 1922; the church was filled with spring flowers and the day brilliant with sunshine as they drove from the church to the reception in a coach and pair.

On August 20th, 1924, their first and only child was born – and christened Peter Nelson Spencer.

As a parent, Beatrice was a strict disciplinarian, as was her own mother. She shared her husband's idealism and sense of fun, however, though perhaps with more reserve. They both had the ability to take the rough with the smooth, and to enjoy the small pleasures of life, which they shared with Peter, who was brought up – always – to count his blessings.

Chapter Two

FOND AS he was of his family, Peter had another reason for spending nearly all his leaves in Wallasey. Since the beginning of 1945 he had been receiving letters almost daily from a very pretty girl in the A.T.S. called Wendy Whitehouse, who had been making steady inroads on his heart. He had known her for about a year and latterly they had met on every leave and gone dancing at the Tower Ballroom, New Brighton, a favourite meeting place, not only for them but for all their friends on leave.

Enid Carlile, the girl vocalist at the Tower, was also a good friend and often sang to him the songs of the day, "When I go for a Walk" and "It Had to be You".

"I had a letter from Enid today, but I assure you we are only friends. After all, I have known her for over seven years," he wrote in one letter to Wendy.

Peter found Wendy so nice to come home to. She was gay and light hearted and laughter came easily to her, although she was going through a very worrying time, her mother being ill with cancer.

"I called to see your mother yesterday," he wrote in January. "She seemed just as cheerful as usual. I notice the wonderful way in which you work for her and make her comfortable. You seem so kind and understanding . . ."

And in February:

"I heard 'My Prayer' on the radio today whilst flying over the Channel... Like you, I hate goodbyes. The times I heard 'When they ask about you' in the air was enough to drive me crazy...

"Last night I went to the Tower, but it wasn't the same without you..."

And in March:

"One of my father's mottoes is 'count your blessings', and the blessing of having your love is something worth counting!"

Although she spent much of her leaves nursing her mother, Wendy still managed to fit in time for parties and dancing, and up until that fateful day in March, she and Peter spent every available minute together.

On February 6th, 1945, Peter was made a Flight Sergeant and in March he took part in the Rhine Crossing. The plan was to drop troops across the Rhine beyond Wesel, several miles behind the enemy's lines, to tie up with the main army who were crossing on the ground. The whole command of Dakotas, comprising over four hundred tug and glider combinations, assembled at various airfields on the east coast of England and stayed there for two nights, preparing for "Operation Varsity".

The glider train was led by Wing Commander R. G. Dutton, Peter's Commanding Officer, later awarded the D.S.O., and Peter's aircraft was number seven. Dawn was just breaking as they took off. It was a wonderful sight. Hundreds of aircraft were lined up at the end of the runway and the gliders brought up by small trucks and hitched to them. As each plane took off the next one followed at a prearranged signal. This was timed to a split second so that all the aircraft taking off from various parts of the country met at a given point and formed one continuous stream. The most nerve-wracking part of the take-off was that if anything went wrong – there was a correct procedure for taking up the slack of the ropes – it would seriously upset the timetable, and therefore the whole operation.

Behind the Dakotas were the Halifaxes and Lancasters, all towing gliders. It was very impressive; the long long stream of aircraft and gliders glistening in the sun as they flew over Southern England and across the Channel.

Peter could see the Rhine a silver streak ahead of him, and beyond it a thick black haze of smoke where Bomber Command had been in before them.

Just as well, he thought. For, as always, they were un-escorted and unarmed. The Dakotas were slow compared with bombers and fighters and there was no chance of escaping from anyone who attacked them either in the air or from the ground.

Flak had already started coming up over the Rhine, but Ken did not have much trouble in finding the points to turn because once the first crew were over the dropping zone he could see fairly clearly. As they approached it, a voice came over the intercom,

"Hello, Tug. We're getting ready to cast off now."

"Cheerio, Matchbox. Good luck," said Peter with feeling as he watched the glider release the cables which held her to the Dakota and they banked off to the right, leaving Matchbox to her fate.

It was an emotional moment, as the air was thick with smoke and dust from Wesel, making it difficult for the gliders to see their objectives, and Peter had already seen two gliders go down in flames.

Their primary concern now was to get to Brussels as quickly as possible. They were supposed to continue a further couple of miles past the dropping zone and then drop their rope, but the flak was getting heavier minute

24

by minute. After they had done about a mile, one shell burst right underneath them and rocked the plane.

"Right! I'm getting the hell out of here," said Smithy. As he did a quick U turn and dropped the rope, a Dakota in front of them went into a spin, flames shot into the air, and the plane hurtled downwards. One parachute floated out and Peter watched it disappear in the smoke.

As they headed back for Brussels the aerial armada was still streaming in behind them, and they saw several go down in flames. It was an awe-inspiring sight: hundreds of aircraft coming in an apparently endless stream which covered twenty or thirty miles.

Once out of the holocaust, Bert had a quick look round and came running up to the front as eager as a schoolboy.

"We've got some holes to take back!" he said, grinning broadly.

They landed at an aerodrome just outside Brussels. They were not given the name, but simply a code number and a map reference. Here they waited. If there was any hitch between the main army meeting up with the paratroopers, they were there ready to fly over supplies and keep them equipped. In fact, their aircraft was actually loaded up with ammunition and shells, but this time it was not necessary. Operations "Varsity", "Plunder" and "Flashpoint" had been a success. Railway lines had been cut, stations wrecked, towns reduced to rubble, two oil refineries put out of action, and hundreds of troops landed successfully across the Rhine, with the Luftwaffe powerless to intervene. The following day 512 Squadron returned to Broadwell.

It was March the 26th.

Chapter Three

MARCH THE 27th was different from the start. But there was nothing to indicate that the day would be engraved on Peter's mind for the rest of his life.

He need not have been on the flight at all. He had just gone along for the trip – because he enjoyed flying – anywhere. It was exactly two years ago to the day that he had joined the R.A.F. and now he was sitting at the piano in the mess playing "When they Ask About You". It was Wendy's favourite tune, and the last time he played it she had been sitting beside him. He smiled to himself, visualising her startled face as he had turned to her and said,

"I'm going to teach you to play the piano."

"But, darling, I can't play a note!"

"It doesn't matter," he had said, imperturbably. "I'll teach you."

"Well . . ." Wendy's pretty face broke into the smile that enchanted him, "You've set yourself an impossible task, but you can try."

That leave seemed a long way away. Peter got up from the piano, walked restlessly across the room, picked up a magazine and dropped into a nearby chair. He was flicking idly through its pages when Smithy breezed in, full of enthusiasm.

"I've volunteered for a special job at Northolt. Hush

hush. Don't know what. Any of you chaps like to come along?"

Peter was on his feet like a shot, followed just as quickly by Ken, but Bert had other fish to fry. He had a date with a very special girl and had no intention of breaking it.

Lucky chap! thought Peter. Wallasey was 150 miles away and he was only able to meet Wendy when their leaves coincided.

"They've given us an Anson," Smithy said, as the three of them walked out to the airfield.

Ken groaned. The Anson was a training aircraft. Small, slow, cumbersome, and of course unarmed, it was used only for short hops, although it could seat half a dozen or more. They flew to Northolt, reported in to control and were told they were to take four officers, a Wing Commander, a Squadron Leader and two Army Majors, to attend a conference at Rheims.

It was a reasonably fine day as they left Northolt and flew towards the coast, but once they reached the Channel heavy cloud began to form, and two-thirds of the way across it started to rain. As they had no navigational equipment, it was impossible to fly above the cloud, so Smithy had to take the Anson down lower, and still lower, to keep beneath it. Deciding it was too risky going into the French coast because of the hills, Smithy took the aircraft right down to the water, but it was raining heavily now and the cloud had come down to the sea, closing them in. It was impossible to see where they were.

"We can't make it. Find somewhere to land," said Smithy.

As they flew towards the English coast looking for a suitable aerodrome, Ken and Peter scanned the maps.

"Ford," said Ken. "It's the first aerodrome going westward."

"Right," Smithy said. "We'll drop in and see what the weather situation is and if it's going to last."

They landed at Ford in Sussex and went up to the Met office in the control tower to look at the weather maps with the meteorologist. He told them it had closed in all round and the flight would have to be postponed.

Deciding to return to Northolt rather than hang about at Ford, they had lunch, and at three o'clock an American truck collected them to drive the seven of them three-quarters of a mile across the airfield to the Anson.

The roof and sides of the truck consisted of steel hoops covered in canvas, and there were wooden forms down either side. The four officers sat on the left hand side of the vehicle, Ken got in first on the other side, near the driver, then Peter and finally Smithy.

They were driving around the perimeter track grumbling about the waste of time when they heard the sound of an aircraft. Ken left his seat and moved to the window, where he stood holding on to the crossbar. Looking out, he could see an aircraft in the distance taxi-ing towards them.

"Only a Mosquito," he said and, turning his back to the window, continued talking as the truck came to a halt.

The next moment there was an ear-splitting crash and the roof caved in. The starboard propeller of the Mosquito tore through the right-hand side of the truck and, taking two or three turns, slashed the canvas, ripped open Smithy's spine, and sliced off Peter's right arm at the shoulder.

Ken struggled out from under the tarpaulin to find the officers already out, as their side had not fully collapsed. Peter's body was lying on the ground, where he had been thrown from the truck by the force of the impact, and for a moment no one realised anything was wrong.

Hearing a muffled voice calling from under the tarpaulin, "My back . . ." Ken jumped into the truck and, with the help of the others, got Smithy out. His back was covered in blood and they lay him on his stomach on the ground and turned to Peter.

With a shock of horror Ken saw Peter's arm lying on the ground, two yards away from his body, the signet ring still on his finger. His jacket was shredded, his eyes greyed over and he could not see, but he was conscious. Ken bent over him.

"I can't feel my arms," Peter said, his voice just a thin thread of sound.

"Don't worry about it now," said Ken reassuringly. "You'll be all right."

Smithy was lying on his face, he didn't know what was wrong with him but he couldn't get up, so he put out a hand and caught hold of someone's trouser leg.

"God," said a shocked voice, "I thought you were dead."

After what seemed an eternity, the ambulance arrived, the two bodies were lifted on to stretchers and, still in a state of shock, Ken picked up Peter's arm from the ground and climbed into the ambulance beside him.

The shock of being moved had caused both Peter and Smithy to lose consciousness. Peter knew nothing of the bumpy ride to Ford R.A.F. Hospital, of the first aid he was given to stop the bleeding, or of the second drive twelve miles down the coast to Chichester. He knew nothing until he regained consciousness in a hospital bed in St. Richard's Hospital in excruciating pain. He was propped up against pillows, his neck swathed in bandages, his right arm gone, his left arm lying heavily bandaged on a pillow.

Peter's first thought was, *I won't be able to play the piano!* It hit him with the force of a hatchet.

Then slowly hope began to rise again. I've got my left hand. There are arrangements for one hand only. I should still be able to play some things..."

Relief flooded through him; till he tried to raise his

left arm. It was powerless, he couldn't move it, not any of it, not even the hand, not even his fingers.

A wave of nausea came over him. No! What had they done to him! The pain was coming through him like a tornado, tearing through the nerves of his body. He was consumed by it. He lost consciousness with one terrible thought in his mind:

I will never be able to play again.

Nelson and Beatrice Spencer first heard the news about their son at seven p.m. on March 27th. They had not been worrying about Peter because, not only did they both possess a strong faith – which they certainly needed in the days to come – but they had received a letter from Peter at four that very afternoon to tell them all was well.

"I nearly sent you a telegram to say I was O.K. but telegrams are pretty scaring things, aren't they? Don't know about leave yet, it's probably been put back a week or two. You can bet I'll be home as soon as possible . . ."

They knew he had been on the Rhine Crossing, and had listened to it on the wireless, but were not really worried, even when they heard the commentator say that one of our aircraft had gone down in flames.

It couldn't be Peter.

But at seven that evening the doorbell rang and Nelson Spencer was handed a telegram, not from their son, but from the Air Ministry. As his wife joined him in the hall, Nelson stared down at the words without comprehension.

"We regret to inform you that your son, Flt. Sgt. Peter Nelson Spencer is critically ill in St. Richard's Hospital, Chichester."

"Critically ill." What did it mean?

30

Beatrice Spencer's mind flew back to an evening over two weeks ago when Peter had been home on sick leave following tonsillitis and they had gone to see "Flare Path", a play about a pilot who had gone out of his mind.

Had Peter been involved in an accident which had affected his mind?

Filled with dread, they caught the ten-thirty train from Liverpool that evening to London and thence to Chichester. It was a nightmare journey in an unheated train with all the inevitable wartime delays and an air raid warning to greet them in London – the very last siren of the war. They sat in the cold and dark at Euston Station and thought of their son. Nelson held his wife's hand and they drew comfort, as they always had done, from each other.

They finally arrived at Chichester at eleven-thirty the following morning, after a sleepless night and a thirteen hour journey. St. Richard's was a brand new hospital, glistening and antiseptic, filled with hurrying nurses, doctors, patients being wheeled on trolleys . . . And nobody took any notice of them. They made their way tentatively to the reception desk and gave their name.

"Oh, I'm glad you've come," said the receptionist. "Your son is in Ward 1."

They made their way, alone, down the long gleaming white corridor, fearful of what they might see. Still, no one had told them what had happened.

It was a small ward and Peter's bed was screened off. He was lying propped up by pillows, his eyes closed, his face haggard and drawn with pain. Beatrice's heart turned over: he looked so ill. Her legs gave way under her and she sat down abruptly on a chair near the bed. They could see Peter's neck swathed in bandages, and his left arm. But his right . . . ?

Peter's eyes opened and he looked at them hazily, for he was heavily drugged against the pain.

31

"Hello, Mum." He tried to smile, but couldn't quite make it.

"Hello, Peter," said Beatrice tremulously. "What's happened?"

"Lost my right arm," he said. "Won't be able to play again." And he drifted away from them; his mind, and the pain, mercifully dulled by the drugs.

Suddenly Beatrice gave a little sob and, as Nelson put a comforting arm around her, her world went black and she slumped forward. The next thing she knew a nurse was standing over her.

"You'd be better outside in the fresh air," she was saying.

So Nelson helped his wife to her feet, and together they went outside. Beatrice sat down on the cold stone step and the tears trickled down her cheeks and she didn't even know she was crying. It was too much to comprehend. It couldn't be real. Nelson sat beside her and tried to comfort her. But what could he say . . .? Where to find words of comfort at a time like this . . .?

Beatrice blew her nose and stood up. "I'm all right," she said firmly. "We'll go back to Peter."

But Peter was still unconscious and while Beatrice sat with him, Nelson went in to see the Matron.

"Please sit down, Mr. Spencer." Matron looked at him as though testing his strength. "I regret having to tell you this, but it is better that you should know the truth. Your son has lost his right arm in an accident on the airfield, his neck has been dislocated, and his left arm paralysed. I think I should warn you that he is not expected to live. In cases like this the patient almost invariably dies of depression."

Nelson looked at her. He heard the words, they beat against the outer wall of his brain, but they did not mean anything. He did not believe them. He refused to believe them.

32

Peter (at the piano) and other trainee pilots enjoy a sing-song in Florida in December 1943.

Early gadgets: *above*, enabli Peter to smoke unaided a *below*, the writing apparatus whi allowed him to write in priva and without help.

He stumbled out of the room. In a low voice he repeated Matron's words to Beatrice, all but the last sentence. He could not tell her now. He could not put a pronouncement of death upon their son.

Eventually they went into the town and found a little restaurant where they ordered a meal. But it was difficult to eat. They returned to the hospital in the afternoon, and again in the evening. In between, they walked the streets of Chichester.

As Beatrice watched over her son, her mind drifted back to the happy past. She saw him trotting beside her down to the shops, an attractive, obedient little boy with a round smiling face, neat and tidy and well turned out in his white linen suit. Or running towards her, with an expression of concern, after going to see a neighbour's new baby.

"Mummy. Baby Alice hasn't got any toys."

"Well, what are you going to do about it?"

He had looked around him, puzzled, until his eyes alighted on his toy box. "I'll give her my new bunny," he said in delight.

"That's a good boy." She patted his three-year-old curly head in approval.

Always share: share your blessings, share your life, share your love. These were the precepts upon which Peter had been brought up.

At seven he was already a handsome child, self-possessed, with straight brows, a direct gaze and a determined look about the mouth and chin. Very reserved at this age, he was highly indignant when having been reluctantly persuaded, to take part in a Sunday School play, he emerged as a page boy resplendent in a white satin suit, and all his friends laughed.

But Peter enjoyed most things: playing the piano, picnics on the beach or in the winter on Bidston Hill, swimming, cricket, football, cycling – even school. He

33

threw himself wholeheartedly into them all. Into everything except the church choir. At this he drew the line.

"But why, Peter?"

"I don't want to. I can't sing, and I'd feel a fool."

"But you should insist," the vicar's wife said later to Beatrice. "The more things he joins in the better. It will help him to overcome his reserve."

"No." Beatrice's mind was made up. "I don't believe in forcing him." And that was the end of that, for, like her son, what Beatrice did not believe in she did not do.

But that was a long time ago. He had grown up fond of sport, a powerful swimmer, a member of the Rugger team, captain of the cricket team and, despite the disruptions of war, had obtained credits in seven subjects and distinction in physics with chemistry in his school certificate exams.

"Intelligent and good at games. In fact a good all rounder," said his schoolmaster. "The type of boy who makes you think you are doing something worthwhile after all, and not always banging your head against a brick wall."

At sixteen Peter had left school and taken a job in the Ministry of Supply to tide him over until he could join up, but his heart was in the Air Training Corps which he joined as soon as it was formed, and in his brief spare time he played the piano. Every evening when he came home he would sit in the dark and play to himself; popular music, classical music, syncopation . . . anything which interested him, but always he would start with "In the Mood". It became his signature tune, and Beatrice would listen from the kitchen where she was preparing the meal and smile to herself. One day perhaps he would be a famous pianist . . . She saw him surrounded by eager faces, she heard the thunder of applause . . . It was a God given talent.

Peter stirred in the hospital bed, he turned his head

restlessly towards her, but his eyes were closed, his face grey with pain, and she saw again the empty sleeve where his arm should be, the inert left hand.

Dear God. Why his hands? Why take it all away?

On Good Friday, Nelson and Beatrice went into the quiet of Chichester Cathedral and knelt and prayed for strength to endure that which seemed unendurable. Above all, they prayed for strength for their son. But, through it all, came the question:

Why . . . Lord?

How to still the question, and to accept? Was there a purpose behind it? It was difficult to see. How could there possibly be. And yet, if one believed . . . there was a purpose behind everything.

So they prayed . . . Not only that their son might live, but that he might rejoice to live.

Chapter Four

For the first week at St. Richard's Hospital, Peter was under heavy sedation. Ken Thwaites came to see him more than once, but Peter heard nothing from the pilot of the Mosquito nor the driver of the truck. Nor did anyone come to visit him in an official capacity. There was never an enquiry, and the cause of the accident was, and still is, unknown.

Peter drifted in and out of consciousness unaware of time, of the days that passed. Only aware of a great sea of pain that tore through him, battering his body and mind, threatening to destroy him.

He was consumed by a terrible sadness. Why did it have to happen? And, having happened, must he go on enduring it? He longed for the blessed needle that brought relief, so that he could escape the physical torture and sink into his dreams. He was vaguely conscious of the nurses bustling about, of people bringing meals which he could not eat, of his parents' kindly faces, strained by grief, but keeping cheerful for his sake. His father even tried to smile. They were brave. It was rotten for them, rotten for everyone . . .

The pain, now, was so terrible he wanted to scream. "Put me out! *Put me out!*"

But there was the nurse, coming towards him, smiling, a hypodermic needle in her hand.

"Here's your shot."

Thank God. Peter closed his eyes and drifted back into a beautiful world where there was no pain, back into his childhood where everything was warm and safe and secure . . .

He was a small boy again trotting beside his mother, going to visit grandma: the treat of the week. Rushing excitedly into the house, calling, "Grandma, we're here! We're here! Have we got trimps for tea?"

Grandma Ingle was smiling down at him. "Yes, of course. We always have shrimps for Peter."

The shrimps were fresh from the sea; Peter could taste them now. The shrimp man had been fishing all night off the coast of New Brighton and brought them straight round by pony and trap.

Sometimes Peter stayed the night, and in the morning he would climb into grandma's bed and snuggle up close while she gave him sips of her tea . . . "Never with sugar! It spoils the taste . . ." and told him exciting stories of conquering heroes. Later, Grandpa Ingle, a quiet man with a heavy moustache and a fine operatic voice, would play to him on the oboe and explain carefully the intricacies of the wireless set he was in the process of making. He was a man of many parts.

When his grandparents moved to Wales, Peter would cycle to see them in their little cottage, Inglenook, which nestled in the foothills of the Welsh mountains. He would never forget his grandmother's indomitable spirit. How proud she was, how self-contained and erect in bearing. She ruled her household with a firm hand, and when Grandpa Ingle died in 1939 she continued to live there alone, cooking splendid meals and baking all her own bread and cakes. Age receded before her resolute tread and unequivocal eye . . .

Peter's face momentarily twisted with pain, involuntarily he cried out, and a cool hand soothed his forehead. That was nice.

37

"It's all right," said a reassuring voice. "You are going to be all right."

Yes. He was going to be all right. Tiny said so. Tiny was wonderful. Nothing was too much trouble for her, his mother said. A Day Sister, yet often she would sit up with him half the night.

Peter's mind drifted away again. Somewhere he could hear a dog barking. Gyp! They were racing together across the golf course, which was open to the public on Sundays, when abruptly Gyp bounded out of sight. As Peter raced after him, he heard a terrible howl of anguish that went right through him. By the time he reached the railway line it was too late. Gyp had squeezed through the gap in the fence and his small body was lying scorched and blackened across the electrified line.

For a long time afterwards the sound of that howl of anguish haunted Peter's dreams. He never had another dog.

Peter opened his eyes and saw his mother's face. She was sitting on a chair by the hospital bed, her hands folded in her lap. She looked so sad, but what could he say to comfort her?

Why had he been so keen to join up? What had propelled him into it? He was sixteen and returning home from fire watching. Behind shuttered lids he saw again the darkened street in Wallasey . . . heard the wail of the sirens . . . the drone of planes overhead . . . the bombs dropping . . . And then, out of a ravaged house, a young woman running, distraught . . .

"My baby . . . Where is my baby . . . ?"

The agony in her voice had caused a sudden fury in him.

"I'll stop this lot coming over!" he vowed.

Well, he had not stopped them, but at least he had helped. Just like that other young pilot in Shropshire, who had paid the full price.

38

Peter saw himself cycling through the sunlit Shropshire countryside. He had just joined up and was having a brief holiday and feeling on top of the world, when suddenly he heard the drone of an aircraft overhead and looked up. It was a Miles Master training plane, flying low; the engine was not spluttering but he knew instinctively that it was in trouble.

The aircraft went over a rise of ground and disappeared behind a hillock. Almost immediately a great plume of black smoke rose into the air. Taking the next turning, Peter raced towards it. There was no sign of a parachute or anyone baling out, it was too low for that. If only he could reach him in time he might be able to help free the pilot.

But he was too late. By the time Peter reached the plane it was already an inferno, lying on its side in a pond, with flames tearing into the sky and, in the debris, Peter could see the pilot's body burning, his half-opened parachute twisted around him.

Several people were already on the spot, but there was nothing any of them could do. The boy was just another casualty of the war.

Peter did not think, This might happen to me. He was too conscious of the surging life inside him to know fear. Death is a stranger to a youth of seventeen. Nevertheless, he refrained from telling his parents. There was no need to worry them unnecessarily.

He stirred in the hospital bed. There were voices around him, bringing him back, unwillingly, to the present. He could not understand what they were saying, and then as though in a sudden silence, he heard quite clearly: "I'm afraid he won't live. He will die of depression."

Who were they talking about? Him! Through half closed lids he saw them grouped around the bed, and a deep anger welled up inside him. Who did they think they were! God? Maybe there had been times when he

39

had wanted to die, when the pain had been unendurable, but he hadn't really meant it. He had no intention of dying. What right had they to pronounce a death sentence upon him?

The voices became blurred and indistinct. They drifted away and Peter was alone, with his dreams and his thoughts and his pain. He knew that from now on he had got to face life like this: armless.

Never again would he be able to handle the controls of an aircraft and feel it respond to his touch, lifting away from the earth into the empty sky; or touch the keys of a piano and feel them reply with the liquid magic of sound. Never again would he hold a cricket bat, and experience the satisfying thwack of the willow against the ball; or put the full power of his body into a fast bowl and watch the ball crack against the wicket. Never again would he dive into the sea and feel the shock of pleasure as his body sliced through the water ...

He shut his eyes tightly. It was no good thinking like that. It was over. He had just got to live from one day to the next, in the best way he could.

Perhaps there were compensations. There must be. When God shut one window he always opened another. But at this moment the window was shrouded over. He could not see through it.

He must learn to face a life of contemplation instead of action. But he was too young to contemplate. He did not want to be on the sidelines, a mere spectator of life at twenty. He was at the peak of his manhood. He wanted to participate!

Peter looked across at the bed on his left where Smithy lay with closed eyes, while his wife sat beside him looking pale and drawn. Smithy was in pretty bad shape, but he still had the use of his limbs, thank God, and with not only a wife but a baby daughter to look after, he would certainly need them.

"If anyone had to lose his arms," said Peter to his mother, "it was better that it should be me."

On April 4th, eight days after the accident, Nelson Spencer had to return to his job with the Mersey Docks and Harbour Board in Liverpool, where he had been employed since 1940. But there was one matter he needed to reassure himself about before he left. Peter never seemed to move his legs. It had gradually been borne in on Nelson that his son might be a quadriplegic, without the use of *any* of his limbs.

His lips hardly dared form the question, but before he went home he must know.

"How are your legs, son?"

"My legs?" Peter looked faintly surprised. "Why, they're fine." Then, seeing his father's worried face, he added, "Want to see?"

"Yes."

"Right!"

Peter gave a mighty kick that practically sent the bed-clothes flying, then he shook them vigorously.

"There! What do you think of that? As fine a pair of legs as you'll see anywhere, Dad. Coming for a hike?"

"Any day now." Nelson grinned at his son; he felt weak at the knees with relief.

As soon as he was strong enough they gave Peter tests for his left arm.

"Well," the doctor stood over the bed smiling down at him. "Not as bad as we thought. It's just shock causing the paralysis. You should have the feeling back in that arm in a couple of weeks' time."

A couple of weeks! Suddenly a window had been opened and Peter could bear to look through it out on to the world again. There were so many things he could do with

41

one arm. At least he would not be completely helpless, dependent upon others for the rest of his life.

His spirits rose enormously. They rose even higher when he received a letter from Wendy to say she had managed to get a seventy-two hour pass and was coming down to Chichester to see him. But his happiness was short-lived. The very next day they told Peter he was being transferred from St. Richard's Hospital to the Princess Mary's R.A.F. Hospital at Halton, Buckinghamshire, eighty miles north, and he had to telegraph Wendy to postpone her visit.

It nearly broke his heart; while the journey to Halton on April 6th nearly broke his spirit. They gave him no injection to dull the pain and for three exhausting hours he was jolted around in an ancient ambulance until every nerve in his body was crying out in agony.

Princess Mary's was the principal hospital of the Royal Air Force and possessed exceptional specialist facilities. It was filled with members of the R.A.F. with every conceivable kind of injury, but throughout his entire hospital career Peter did not come across another individual who had lost the use of his arms. On the surface he joked and made light of his troubles with the others, but underneath he experienced a growing sense of isolation.

Three days after his admission to the R.A.F. Hospital they enclosed Peter in a plaster jacket, a cumbersome thing that enveloped him from chin to waist, including his left arm which was bent at right angles to his body. The weight of the jacket hanging from his shoulders was almost unbearable.

He sat propped up in bed rather like an unfinished Egyptian mummy; weak, powerless, and in constant pain, unable to move on his own or do anything to pass the weary hours. It was about this time that he started receiving cheering letters from his friends, all of whom,

42

almost without exception, finished up with, "Never mind, old boy. Keep your chin up."

Peter smiled wryly. He had little option!

A good deal of joking went on in the wards, some of it slightly macabre. On one occasion an R.A.F. Sergeant who had lost a leg was about to make his first foray into Aylesbury. As he hopped down the ward on crutches, one bright spark who had lost both legs shouted after him:

"You there! Get properly dressed before you go out. Fasten your top button. Where's your cap? Where's your left leg?"

The sergeant gave a wry grin and most of the ward burst into laughter. Such incidents helped to lighten the atmosphere. But there was one episode which stuck grimly in Peter's memory when he felt very far from laughter.

A well meaning padre came into the ward trundling a piano in front of him and, positioning it carefully at the foot of Peter's bed, he sat down and began to play loudly and with enthusiasm.

Peter lay rigid in his bed, taut with misery. Every chord beat on his brain like a hammer blow, reminding him of all that he had lost. A silent scream ran through his body, *Get out!* GET OUT!

But, totally unaware of his feelings, the padre continued to play, until at last Peter blocked his mind to the sound and lay there numb, without hearing. To withdraw his mind was his only defence, and one which he was to use on many occasions.

When Peter was moved to Halton, Beatrice Spencer went to stay with her sister-in-law, Mary, at Hatfield in Hertfordshire. From here they would make the journey every two or three days to visit Peter. It was nearly thirty miles cross country and involved three different buses, so after a fortnight of this it was suggested that Beatrice should stay at the Red Cross Hostel in Halton.

Never liking to be idle, when she was not feeding Peter and keeping him company, Beatrice offered her services to the Red Cross.

Peter had no interest in food at all and for many weeks existed almost solely on Mars Bars and milk. Friends and relations saved up their sweet coupons and sent them to him.

There is an art in feeding, and most of the nurses who were rushed off their feet, had little time to perfect it. Also their fingers often smelled of disinfectant and, to Peter, a quick glass of milk and two or three bites of a Mars Bar were preferable to the long drawn out business of being fed war time meat and veg. mouthful by mouthful.

Although Peter was up now and walking around, he could not walk far in his weakened condition because of the weight of the plaster jacket. He could, of course, do nothing for himself; his toilet requirements, shaving, washing, dressing, all had to be done for him. He could not hold a book or turn its pages, light a cigarette or blow his nose.

Peter had received several letters from Wendy but, as he was unable to write to her except through someone else, correspondence was difficult. And Wendy's visits to Peter were restricted by the fact that she had her mother to look after, whose cancer had now become serious.

However, early in May, Peter received a letter to say Wendy was coming down to see him on May 7th. He looked forward to the day with excitement mixed with trepidation. How would she react to the sight of him encased in a plaster jacket – a man with one arm gone and the other useless?

44

Chapter Five

WENDY CAME into Ward 6 of Princess Mary's Hospital like a ray of spring sunshine. Peter felt better from just looking at her, in fact the whole ward brightened up. She laughed and chatted with him almost as if nothing had happened; there were moments when he began to wonder if it had. She fed him a poached egg and treated it as a joke; she held his hand at frequent intervals, asking with her delightful smile, "Now! Can you feel my hand now?"

Peter shook his head.

"Are you sure?"

"I can't feel anything."

"Well, you will soon, I'm positive."

Her gay optimism was infectious. The hospital had said two weeks: in two weeks he would have the feeling back in his hand and arm. Now, they were saying it might take longer: perhaps several months. The nerves had been damaged by the dislocation of the neck, but already he was having physiotherapy treatment for his hand, and as soon as he was out of the plaster jacket they could start on his arm.

Wendy was wholly optimistic. Because of the plaster jacket it was not obvious that Peter's right arm was missing, and his left was, apparently, only temporarily impaired. Apart from this, he was a whole man. He was surrounded by men with damaged limbs, broken legs, amputated legs, fractured ribs. They were all in the best

45

possible hands. They were all going to get better. This was Wendy's reasoning. It was encouraging after the sorrow that had surrounded him.

May 8th was VE Day. Peter went into Aylesbury with Wendy and his mother, wearing a vivid pink pyjama jacket on top of his trousers – the only garment he possessed which would go over the plaster jacket. Also, it seemed fitting for the occasion, for it was the end of the war with Germany – a day of rejoicing.

In the evening he went out for a drink with the boys and, afterwards, everyone congregated in the square and there was singing and laughter and an excess of high spirits. Most of the boys Peter was with knew that they were going to recover; they could return to their old jobs, or start new ones, picking up the threads where they had left off.

But, for Peter, victory had come too late. Had the war ended six weeks earlier he could have rejoiced too; but now – what did the future hold for him? In the middle of the laughter he was conscious of an overwhelming sadness.

The following day Wendy returned to Wallasey and Beatrice went with her. Peter was on his own. His spirits went down and his desire for food vanished altogether. He lay in bed with nothing to do and no one to talk to, in constant pain and discomfort, rejecting any food which was put before him.

So, ten days later they sent for Beatrice, and she returned and devoted the next six weeks to sustaining Peter's spirit and encouraging him to eat enough to retain his strength.

One of the few other people Peter would take food from was a girl called Laura Derbyshire, the Administrative Sergeant. A happy, friendly girl with a warm smile, she had, in common with all the medical staff, a tremendous admiration for Peter's courage, and considered it an honour to be permitted to feed him.

Soon after VE Day Smithy turned up at Halton. Peter was pleased to see him and, being a convivial outgoing type, Smithy soon made a niche for himself in the ward. His spine had been fractured, several ribs damaged and one lung had collapsed, so for the last month he had been at King Edward's Sanatorium, Midhurst, but he took it fairly philosophically and considered himself lucky compared with some of the others in the ward.

During the third week in June one of the doctors approached Peter with a smile on his face.

"Well, old chap, we're going to take that jacket off you today."

"Marvellous!" Peter's eyes lit up. He was enchanted at the thought of losing the heavy, smelly thing; while having a bath after his ten week incarceration would be sheer heaven. He sank back on to the bed exultant. A free man at last!

But not for long. Before he had time to get used to the idea they had him back in the plaster room again.

"Just a small one this time, old man," said the doctor. "Be much better for you."

He dipped a wide plaster of paris bandage in water and, wrapping it round Peter's neck, left it to set until it became as hard as concrete.

Peter felt as if he were being strangled. He was unable to move his head, and the weight of the collar on his wasted shoulders was agonising. He endured it for a few days but he gradually became so depressed that Beatrice tackled one of the surgeons about it.

"What did he say?" asked Peter when she returned to the ward.

"He said it had nothing to do with the collar, that deep depression is inevitable in a case such as yours, and that the depression will gradually get worse, not better."

"Oh, *did* he!" Peter's expression changed and the light of battle came into his eyes. The hell he did, he thought. What does he know about it.

And from that moment he gradually pulled himself out of his lethargy and depression and began to fight back. It was Peter's spirit over these next few months that kept his parents going.

At the end of that week, to his immense relief, he was taken out of the collar. Then followed a concentrated course of physiotherapy and electrical treatment on the paralysed arm and hand in an endeavour to keep his muscles active and stimulate movement in the hope of eventual recovery.

On July 3rd, four months after the accident, to his great delight, they allowed Peter to go home for the first time. He lived, and usually slept, in his parents' house in Wallasey, and was driven in daily to The Lees, a convalescent home in Hoylake, Cheshire, where his treatment continued, apart from three weeks in August when he returned to Halton where he celebrated his twenty-first birthday.

It was, of course, wonderful to be away from the atmosphere of hospitalisation and sleep at home in his own bed, just as it was wonderful to see Wendy again. She managed to get some leave, but it was a sorrowful time for Wendy as her mother died on July 11th, and Peter shared her sorrow.

During these months Peter started meeting many of his old friends again. To all who knew Peter the news of his accident had come as a great shock. Campbell McRae, one of his oldest friends, met Peter for the first time when he arrived home on leave. For a moment Campbell scarcely recognised him. He was prepared for the missing right arm and the other bound in bandages, but what really struck him to the heart was the terrible thinness and strained paleness of Peter's face, the all too obvious evidence of the pain and suffering he had been through and the closeness to death that he had experienced.

And yet even at that first meeting Campbell noticed how it was Peter who strove from the beginning to put him at his ease and by sheer effort of will forced Campbell to realise that he had accepted what had happened to him and was not going to let it stop him from resuming his life where he had left off.

"During the next few months, as I spent more time in his company," says Campbell, "I noticed over and over again as he renewed old friendships and made new ones, how Peter made so much effort to help others to overcome any awkwardness that they may have felt at meeting him. The way he put them at their ease, accepting help easily and naturally when necessary, managing alone whenever possible, made it easy for people to accept him back into society on his own very independent terms.

"This was the first battle that he had to fight – and to fight at a time when he was still weakened from the ordeal he had been through – still suffering, as he did in those days, a great deal of pain. That he had the courage to fight at all at this time is enough to awaken the greatest admiration for him.

"It was this effort of will and determination, I suppose, that set the pattern for all he was to achieve later. I can remember well the first evening we spent together – the difficulties he had in those early days in doing simple things like opening doors, the first tentative attempts to sort out gramophone records with his feet or carry a few photographs across the room with his teeth as we chatted of old times."

One of the things Peter found most difficult to cope with in those days when he was still in uniform with his arm in bandages was the pitying or curious stares of strangers. One sentiment which Peter did not require was pity. He needed acceptance and independence, or any

49

kind of help which could further his independence. But pity – never.

Once when he was having tea in a restaurant with his mother and she raised the cup to his lips, he heard two women behind them using, all too audibly, the stereotyped phrases that he had heard so often.

"Poor thing."

"Tut, tut."

"Isn't it shocking. Both arms."

"And so young too."

"I don't think they ought to bring him out like that."

"One day," Peter said to his mother in a fury, "I'll turn round and pull tongues at them!"

His courtesy was too inborn for him to put such a threat into practice, but it would have given him a grim satisfaction to see their startled faces.

The other type Peter found hard to take was the individual with a "second cousin in Australia" who had lost a hand or a foot, whereupon he had to stand and listen to the bleak details. A relatively patient man, his patience was sometimes exhausted.

One day a cheerful young face peered round Peter's door. It was David Airey, the ten year old son of a family friend.

"Hello! I thought maybe you'd like me to write some letters for you."

"That's a very nice thought," said Peter with a smile. "It would certainly be a help."

So, every Saturday morning for quite a while young David would arrive armed with pen and paper and write letters in a careful script to Peter's friends, and in particular to Wendy.

Although Peter greatly appreciated this help, he was obviously restricted in the things he was able to say through a second person. But this was only one of the many frustrations he was endeavouring to get used to.

50

Despite the fact that Wendy was very busy at this stage at an Army Transit Camp, she had some leave early in August and she and Peter went out together, visiting friends and to the theatre. But by this time Peter felt in his heart that it was over between them. Nothing was said, there were no "goodbyes", but in November Peter was sent to the Loughborough Rehabilitation Unit in Leicestershire and although he came home for Christmas and he and Wendy met at parties, it was only as friends, one of many; there was no special link between them anymore.

Whether their story would have ended differently if there had been no accident no one can say. Peter accepted the fact as he was learning to accept so many things. On the surface he kept cheerful but inwardly he could not see a ray of light in the bleak future which stretched before him.

The year 1946 moved slowly forward. In February Peter was promoted to Warrant Officer, although this made very little difference to him apart from the fact that he received a small increase in pay.

Housed in the sick quarters of the Loughborough Unit and unable to take part in the games or remedial gymnastics with which most of the other patients occupied their day, Peter was largely thrown back upon his own resources. Every day he visited the physiotherapy department for treatment. He became very friendly with a nursing orderly there called Clarice who helped to brighten what otherwise might have been many empty and lonely hours, for the fact that Peter was without the use of his arms did not appear to lessen his attraction as a man.

In June Peter was transferred from Leicestershire to the Collaton Cross Rehabilitation Unit nearly two hundred miles away in Devon. Clarice visited him there several times, but their friendship came to an end soon after he made his final move to the R.A.F. Rehabilitation Unit in Chessington, Surrey.

Once at Chessington, Peter directed the whole of his mind and energies towards the goal which had always been before him – the achievement of independence.

The Rehabilitation Unit consisted of barrack huts set amongst lawns and paths and Peter, as always, was housed in the sick quarters and looked after by a male orderly. This segregated him from the others who slept in dormitories and spent many hours in the gym. In those days there was no occupational therapy section. Peter sometimes went out with them for a drink at night but as he was unable to join in a game of darts or snooker he tended to spend much of his time reading.

It would have been so easy to retreat from life, just to sit back and let everything be done for him, but this was to admit defeat, to abandon life. Peter's way was to accept and adapt, to swim with the tide, not against it, but constantly to seek new ways in which to develop his strength and skill, so that he would be ready to cope with each new problem as it arose.

One bright morning the M.O. came into the sick quarters dangling a thin aluminium rod or "arm" attached to a padded shoulder.

"I've got something here for you," he said. "Let's try it on for size."

And he proceeded to fit this gadget across Peter's right shoulder, for there was nothing left of Peter's right arm to which anything could be fitted.

"Now, we just pull this strap across the front and button it on to your trousers, and do the same at the back, and there you are! It's got a ballpoint pen fitted to the end so that you can write." The M.O. beamed at him. "Have a go!"

"I feel like a trussed turkey," said Peter, but he had a go.

When sitting at a table, the twelve inch rod sloped down from his shoulder at an angle and the pen was fitted upright into a small clamp at the end. By slowly easing his shoulder back and forward, which required considerable effort, Peter found that eventually he could do a kind of spidery writing.

"That's grand!" he said. "Now I can have a voluminous correspondence."

Peter's first letter was to his parents, and began:

"This is not being written by a small child. It's me!...."

The arm of course was only to use for writing, and even for this did not give Peter complete independence as he still had to ask someone to put the gadget on and take it off for him.

Nevertheless it was encouraging, as this was the first attempt that had been made to rehabilitate him to a life without arms. It had gradually become obvious to Peter that the chances of his ever getting the complete movement back in his left arm and hand were extremely remote. They had explained to him that the fractured neck had caused a brachial plexus lesion. The nerves had been torn apart at the back of the neck between the fifth and sixth cervical, where it resembled an exceptionally complicated telephone exchange with thousands of little wires torn out of their sockets.

Every few months throughout these years Peter was taken to the Wingfield Morris Orthopaedic Hospital in Oxford to see Professor (now Sir Herbert) Seddon for examination. This included electromyography, an electrical method introduced at the beginning of the war to detect signs of recovery in muscles, whereby very small currents indicative of re-innervation can be picked up well in advance of the first feeble flicker of voluntary power. If the nerve roots in the neck were not totally ruptured, then there was hope of spontaneous recovery

53

taking place through new nerve fibres growing down into the paralysed muscles and the insensitive skin. This is, however, a very slow process as the rate at which nerve fibres regenerate is not, on average, more than one and a half millimetres a day.

Because so much depended upon the recovery of Peter's left arm, he was watched with anxious care. The medical people did everything in their power to encourage muscle recovery, but owing to the nature of the injury it was impossible to operate and repair the damaged roots of the brachial plexus.

The M.O. at the Chessington Unit had also devised a gadget consisting of a leather strap fastened around Peter's left wrist to which was attached an eight inch strip of wire with a clamp at the end to hold a cigarette. By bending his head slightly Peter could smoke unaided, and avoid the danger of having the lighted end suddenly put between his lips, as had happened in the past.

After two years of physiotherapy he was just able to bend his arm with the biceps, by swinging it, but was unable to straighten it with the triceps. It simply went straight by gravity. There was no movement in his hand at all.

Throughout these years Peter received a great deal of help from everyone he came in contact with: in hospitals, in rehabilitation units, and of course from parents and friends. But he appeared to be unique. Not once during that time did he meet another person who had lost the use of both arms. He felt that, had he done so, they might have spurred each other on to devising ways and means of coping with the problem. As it was, the Rehabilitation Units had little previous experience of dealing with a situation such as his.

It was his continual total dependence upon others which Peter found so weakening to the morale. He was learning that most of his other losses could be compen-

sated for to some extent – even music. Instead of playing
the piano, he deliberately made himself listen to others
play, until he could do so with pleasure instead of anguish.
Instead of playing cricket, he made himself watch it –
without envy. In fact, he rejoined the Old Boys' Cricket
Club of Oldershaw School as a non-playing but very
active member and presented them with the Spencer
Trophy Cup to be awarded to the cricketer of the
year.

Peter's second step towards independence occurred
when P.5 Branch of the Air Ministry came into his life.
This was a small Branch whose function was the resettlement and rehabilitation of R.A.F. personnel who were
leaving or being invalided out of the service.

The Branch worked in close liaison with the Disablement Resettlement Officers of the Ministry of Labour
and various other bodies. Squadron Leader A. L. S.
O'Beirne and Squadron Leader W. F. Danton who were
jointly responsible for the disabled members, both took
a keen personal interest in the hundreds of men they
endeavoured to launch back into civilian life.

Peter first met Squadron Leader O'Beirne at Loughborough, but it was not until he reached the Chessington
Unit that it was possible to take effective steps to find a
job for Peter when he left the shelter of the rehabilitation
units and stepped out in the competitive atmosphere of
the world again.

At the close of the war Peter had received a letter from
Cambridge asking him whether he would like to return
to Pembroke College when he left the R.A.F. They were
at that time unaware of his disability. Peter had discussed
the possibility with Squadron Leader O'Beirne while at
Loughborough. At that stage, however, only a few
months after his accident, he had not developed the self
confidence to embark upon such an undertaking. It would
have meant a man constantly in attendance to see to all

55

his requirements, and the difficulties then seemed insuperable.

But there were times later when Peter regretted his decision – when he had learnt how often, with sufficient determination, grit and ingenuity, the apparently insoluble problem could be, if not walked through, then certainly walked around.

Squadron Leader O'Beirne, or "Pop" as he liked to be called, was a father figure, a big, roundish, kindly man who had served in the first world war.

He breezed into the sick quarters at Chessington and sat down beside Peter.

"Well, Spencer old boy, what are we going to do with you? What would you *like* to do?"

"I'd like," said Peter, "to become a useful member of the community again. But how?"

So they discussed this at great length and finally came to the conclusion that the one thing that Peter could utilise was his voice.

"We'll fix you up with a course at the Central School of Speech Training and Dramatic Art, and then see what can be done, old chap. Maybe something at the B.B.C. How would you like that?"

Peter thought he might like that quite well. He did not look at the drawbacks; they could be faced when the occasion arose.

So, three times a week for the next six months, Peter was driven to the school of dramatic art in London. He found it a most interesting experience. It was his first venture alone into the outside world, and it did wonders for him. He sat amongst budding eighteen year old Laurence Oliviers and Elizabeth Taylors, learning microphone technique, breath control, how to throw his voice, and similar matters; and the students were, without exception, most understanding and helpful to this man without arms in their midst.

Peter gained a great deal of confidence not only from the course but from getting out and mixing with total strangers. He became friendly with several of the students as well as an attractive and helpful young teacher called Betty Shaw whom he took to see "Oklahoma" at Drury Lane.

It was while he was taking this course that Peter applied for a job as a B.B.C. announcer. Arriving at the auditioning studios in London, he was shown into an enormous room containing a table and a microphone, and left completely alone.

Suddenly a voice boomed through a loudspeaker.

"Right, Mr. Spencer! Will you read the News Bulletin which is in front of you."

Peter looked at it slightly appalled. The Bulletin seemed to be composed almost entirely of foreign names: Japanese, Russian, Portuguese. But he journeyed through it. Next he was asked to announce an impromptu programme of music. This was relatively easy. He sat back as the producer returned to the room, and smiled hopefully at him.

"Your voice came over very well," he was told. "But we are afraid the difficulties would be insuperable. You see, you would frequently be called upon to make last minute alterations to the script; it is necessary to turn pages, move switches, and so on. We are so sorry . . ."

So Peter was back where he started.

Squadron Leaders O'Beirne and Danton had met many serious types of disability through the war years, but this was the greatest challenge they had yet to face. Anyone, in their experience, who had lost the complete use of his hands might be forgiven for thinking he was finished, certainly as far as a career was concerned. But this was something Peter was not prepared to accept; and if he was not, then nor were they. They left no stone unturned in their efforts to find some way in which Peter could utilise his remaining assets in the business world. Countless approaches were made to kind and valuable contacts, innumerable letters written to firms and organisations, and finally their efforts were rewarded. O'Beirne received a reply to a letter he had written to a film company called D.U.K., saying they were prepared to employ Peter as a publicity agent.

For this, he would require both a full-time attendant cum driver and a car. After a lengthy search, Squadron Leader Danton contacted an ex-R.A.M.C. ambulance driver, and he and Peter met at the Air Ministry.

The scheme was discussed at some length. Peter described the job and the type of duties that would be involved in attending to the needs of an armless man. He then explained the financial terms and the rate at which he himself was to be paid, ending with, "Well, there it all is, and if I get a ten bob rise, you'll have half."

"Right," said his driver. "You're on!"

The next hurdle was the acquisition of a car, and it was here that the R.A.F. Benevolent Fund* stepped in. Danton, as the Service member and liaison officer on the Disablement Committee of the Fund, was able to provide every detail of the case for their consideration. The project received their blessing, a car was provided, and Peter stepped forth, inexperienced and unarmed, to do battle on behalf of the film world.

D.U.K. stood for "Do You Know", as the company was originally formed for the purpose of making educational films. They were now, however, acting as distributors for classic feature films, and it was Peter's job to get advance publicity for these by persuading suitable shops to display posters and placards advertising the film. There was usually a tie up: "The Hurricane" would be advertised in a rainwear shop and "The Little Foxes" in a fur shop.

* A voluntary body administered with imagination and elasticity, which is devoted to meeting cases of hardship and need amongst R.A.F. personnel past and present, and their dependants, who have problems which are outside the scope of State assistance.

But, try as he might, Peter could not take to it, nor did it seem to him commonsense to have two men doing what he considered to be one man's job. He could not convince himself that he was serving a useful purpose. So when the driver, who was divorced with a small child, informed him that he was planning to re-marry and provide a home for his daughter, Peter greeted the news more with relief than despair. They parted company and Peter returned home.

In one sense he was back at the starting point. In another he had made an advance for from each contact with the outside world he gained a little more confidence.

On September 18th, 1948, Peter, now twenty-four, was demobbed on the grounds that he "no longer fulfilled the physical requirements of the Royal Air Force".

The understatement of the year! thought Peter grimly. He was awarded the usual one hundred per cent war disability pension of 45s a week, plus allowances.

Although it was perfectly reasonable and he expected it, the reception of his discharge combined with the folding up of the only job which the business world had to offer him, temporarily winded Peter. Now he was really on his own.

Chapter Six

PETER'S SPIRITS went down, and he hung around listlessly for a while just killing time and wondering what was the point of it all. Many hours were spent listening to the radiogram his parents had given him for his twenty-first birthday, and which he operated with his foot; or in reading. Newspapers and magazines he read on the floor, turning the pages with his toes, but books were more of a problem and his mother usually turned the pages of the library books he read every week.

This was only one of the innumerable things she did for him. Both his parents exhausted themselves physically and emotionally – but gladly – on his behalf; for he had to be washed, shaved, dressed, fed, and of course all his personal requirements seen to. Whatever he wanted to do, someone had to help him to do it.

Nevertheless, he always looked immaculately turned out. Because he was forced to lead such a sedentary life, Peter always made himself take at least one good walk a day, whether he felt like it or not. He would go down to the beach, or to Wallasey village or through some of the hundreds of intersecting suburban roads that he knew by heart. Sometimes he crossed the River Mersey to Liverpool and on a clear day if he stood high on a windswept hill, he could gaze west to the mountains and valleys of Wales, through which once he had been able to cycle.

Peter still experienced considerable pain, not only in

the left arm and hand but also in the amputated right –
the phantom limb – a shooting pain down the arm and a
nagging, burning sensation in his fingers as though they
had been plunged in hot oil. He could still feel his non-
existent hand and mentally move his right arm around.
There were times when it was more painful than others;
he could feel the fingers gripping and be unable to release
the grip. The existent fingers of his left hand were hyper-
sensitive; the slightest touch on them was unpleasant, and
there was one particular spot beneath the right armpit
which was so sensitive that he nearly screamed out if
anyone touched it.

It would have been easy in those days to become a drug
addict, but Peter was not the type from which addicts
are made. He resisted the temptation for, after all, any
drug only gave temporary relief; once the effect had
worn off the pain revived with its original intensity. So he
bore it in silence. It had become part of his philosophy
never to show that he was in pain.

It would not have been surprising if Peter had become
a recluse at this stage and withdrawn from the world:
from the stares, the questions and the endless strangers
who offered to shake his hand.

"I'm sorry ... The war, you know," he would say,
hoping to spare them embarrassment. Then, if they
offered the left hand, he would smile and proffer his
elbow – anything to put them at ease.

Peter was acutely conscious of being different, of being
set apart from the others. Nevertheless he was determined
to step off his island; determined to become accepted
again as a normal man. There was nothing dramatic
about his resolution, no bombast at all. But despair was
foreign to his nature, and one bright morning early in
1949, his natural buoyancy of spirit reasserted itself.

Right! he decided. If the R.A.F. were unable to do

anything more for him, then he would carve out a career for himself.

They had intimated that his voice was his only commercial asset, he had been given a training, and now he would put that training to good use.

How? By giving elocution lessons.

The thought was slightly daunting, but once he had made up his mind, he stuck to it.

Naturally, Peter discussed the matter with his parents first, for whatever he did affected them too.

"If I have children here to teach, do you think they will understand?"

"I'm sure they will," said Beatrice. "They might stare at first, but they'll soon take you for granted." And she was right.

Peter's first pupil was a young boy called Billy. He stared at Peter thoughtfully for a full minute.

"What happened to your arms?"

"Oh," Peter looked at him with mock seriousness. "I used to bite my nails as a little boy, and this is the result."

The boy grinned. "You're having me on." From that moment Peter was accepted. No more questions were asked.

Peter's next pupil solemnly announced on her first day, "I've come for electrocution."

Many of the pupils were sent to him by parents who wanted them to lose their Merseyside accents, and the lesson would go somewhat like this:

"Say, 'I like currant buns', John."

"I like coorunt boons."

"No. Take it slowly: currant buns."

A big intake of breath, then victoriously, "Coorunt booons."

"We'll start again . . ." Peter would say patiently. It took a little time, but they got it right in the end!

One of Peter's pupils went in for the Poetry Speaking

Competition at the Music Festival. He arrived on Peter's doorstep one day in a state of great excitement and announced, "Mr. Spencer, I've come in second! If I'd come in first Dad would have given me ten bob."

"Congratulations!" said Peter. "What did he give you for coming second?"

"Oh." The boy's face fell. "Nothing. I didn't have it each way."

His father was, in fact, a bookie.

As the pupils were few in number, especially at the beginning, Peter also decided to offer coaching in arithmetic and English. It was something constructive to do and it brought in a little pin money to augment his meagre pension; but he certainly had no income tax problems!

However, Peter found that despite being demobbed he had not been forgotten by Department P.5. Whenever he was in the area, S/Ldr. Danton would go out of his way to call on him.

"Hello, my boy. How are you getting on?" And whatever the demands on his time, Danton would stay for a chat. His interest and friendliness came from the heart, while his admiration for Peter's gallant and enterprising spirit was unbounded, and he was anxious to help in any way he could. Therefore, when on one of his visits in 1950 he realised how much more Peter could achieve if he possessed a tape recorder, Danton lost no time in putting the idea into action, and in due course one was supplied. It was, in fact, one of the first tape recorders in Wallasey.

Peter found this an invaluable aid in demonstrating to his pupils their good and bad points. At this stage Peter had to have someone thread the tape on for him before the lesson began, but after that he was quite independent. For he had discovered that there are many substitutes for hands. He used the same tape throughout the lesson, wiping it off, rewinding and re-recording as necessary. By

63

balancing on his left leg he could switch the tape recorder on and off with his right foot. By moving his body so that his left elbow was correctly placed, he could use it to push the lever on top of the machine into the right position for rewind, record, playback, and so on.

With patience and constant application – as in all the tasks he tackled – Peter eventually managed, by having the machine on the floor, to go through the whole procedure unaided, including threading the tape from one spool to the other. And, as with everything he achieved, it was carried out so unobtrusively that it had the appearance of a normal action; that is if one had time to notice, so swiftly was it done.

The tape recorder was particularly useful in the case of two pupils whom Peter was to help considerably. One was a middle-aged man who came to him after suffering a stroke, as the result of which his speech was so gravely affected that he was unable to follow his occupation. Peter accepted the challenge gladly. His pupil was taught correct breathing, encouraged to speak slowly and clearly, given special exercises with vowel sounds and consonants:

"Betty Botter bought a bit of butter – but the butter Betty Botter bought was bitter!"

He was taught to bring the corners of his lips closely together for "oooo", "oo oo" and open his mouth as wide as possible for "aaaaah", and given special reading exercises. After some time and considerable effort on both sides, the man's diction was so improved that he was actually able to return to his old employment.

So Peter, a man who with less determination might have resigned himself to a life of total dependence, now found himself in the position of being able to rehabilitate others.

Peter's other outstanding pupil was a girl with a cleft palate. With patience and perseverance he gradually

On honeymoon, Peter and June stroll by the river at Stratford-on-Avon.

June, Robin and Jill in August, 1962.

Photo by Albert Marrion

improved her diction, but that in itself, Peter felt, was insufficient.

"Now," he said one day, "there's nothing to stop you going out and getting yourself a job."

"But," she looked frightened. "I couldn't."

"Why not?"

"People would laugh at me. They would stare."

"Your speech is as good as many people's," said Peter, 'And if they stare – what of it? You'll get used to it. I did."

She looked at him, and then nodded. "Yes, I'm being a coward. If you could face them, then I can, too. There's nothing really to be frightened of."

"Nothing at all."

So she applied for a job as secretary, went for the interview, and to her surprise and pleasure was selected from four others.

"Now," said Peter, "you must broaden your horizons, make some new friends, join an organisation."

"Oh, no, I . . ." She stopped. Peter was smiling at her.

"Yes—?" he questioned, and paused.

"I could, couldn't I? There's nothing to stop me, except myself."

"Exactly," said Peter.

Shortly after that she joined the Young Conservatives, and eventually became a very active member, making a host of new friends in the process.

So many people had helped Peter that it gave him a deep satisfaction to be able, in his turn, to help others.

Feeling that all known means of communication with the outside world were essential to his continuing independence, Peter had already rigged up a telephone which he could use without assistance. He had the receiver fixed to the wall, and arranged a system of pulleys operated by foot, whereby, when a weight was lifted off the

65

base of the phone, he was put in direct contact with the operator.

When the dialling system was introduced to Wallasey the G.P.O. installed a gadget which, when he pressed a button with his chin, would automatically dial 100 and he could then ask the operator for the number he required. But there were several disadvantages to this.

"Have you tried to obtain the number yourself?" the operator would ask.

And Peter had to explain: No, he was disabled.

Then he discovered that by dialling the number himself, it cost only 2d instead of 3d by the box method, and so he abandoned this. He used his mouth to lift off the weight, and with a pencil held in his teeth he dialled the number required. Not only was this quicker and cheaper, but he usually obtained a better line.

Soon after being demobbed, Peter had joined the Liverpool branch of BLESMA, The British Limbless Ex-Service Men's Association and attended their monthly meetings.

A nation wide voluntary body dedicated to the care of war amputees, BLESMA has over a hundred branches, runs three residential homes, acts as a negotiating body for the improvement of war disability pensions and allowances, and unites limbless ex-service men and women in comradeship and service.

When they heard of the physical difficulties Peter encountered in trying to read a book, BLESMA stepped in.

One morning early in 1950, the organising secretary arrived at Grove Road carrying a small machine.

"This ought to make your life a bit easier, Peter," he said, putting the machine on the table and plugging it into the electricity supply. "You just fix a tab to each page, press a button with your foot, and this little rotating hub turns the pages of your book for you. You're one of

66

the first ex-servicemen to try it out. I'll be interested to hear how you get on."

Peter was of course delighted, and most appreciative of their efforts. But there was one snag. Although it simplified the task of page turning, he was still dependent upon someone to put the tabs on the hundreds of pages of each book he read. It still did not give him the longed for independence towards which he was constantly striving. From the moment he left the rehabilitation units, his life had become dedicated to that single goal.

Though the days passed slowly, Peter's evenings were usually occupied, for he was never short of good friends. He played canasta with his life-long friend Campbell McRae, Ken Campbell, who was later to become his brother-in-law, Don Tew and Tony Jones, using a special board in which to stand the cards, and picking them up with his mouth when needed.

He also enjoyed strolling down to the local and engaging in a lively discussion with his pals, including Bill Lloyd and his wife Philli Willi, a derivation of Phyllis Williams, whose uncle Billy Williams was founder of the Twickenham Rugby Ground, affectionately known as "Billy Williams Cabbage Patch". They were both several years older than Peter, but Phyllis was always cheerful, warmhearted and gay, and Bill, a frank and forthright character, liked nothing better than a well informed argument about the affairs of the world. Both of them took a great interest in the progress he was making.

Peter found that the glass or two of beer, the stimulating chat with his friends, the breath of air on the walk back home, seemed to relax him and helped him to sleep more easily.

Despite all this, there was still a great gap of emptiness in his life. He still had only a handful of pupils, there were still many barren hours to be passed somehow. He felt very keenly that his life lacked purpose.

67

Chapter Seven

PETER NEVER knew what directed his steps to New Brighton Pier that day. It was July 12th, 1950 and he had never been on the Pier before. There was a show called "Happy Time" playing in the open air theatre and as he strolled towards it a girl was singing "O, my Beloved Father".

It was her voice which first attracted him; it had enormous depth and range, a very beautiful and unusual voice. He stood at the back of the audience listening, and then became aware of the girl herself. He could not see the colour of her eyes, but it was as though she had a light burning inside her, her hair in the sun was the colour of honey and her personality glowed. He stood watching and listening until she left the stage and, as she walked away, she turned and smiled at him.

When the show was over, Peter remained at the back, waiting. He had not really been conscious of the rest of the show... The audience gradually dispersed, and he moved to the rail and stood gazing out at the sea.

As June Lynette walked off the stage she saw the manager standing in the wings. He looked at her shining eyes and flushed cheeks.

"What's happened?"

June shook her head. "I—don't know ... I feel strange ... I—I've just seen the man I'm going to marry."

She looked at him in astonishment. The words had

68

come out without her fully realising what she was saying. Then, still somewhat bemused, she went to change.

When June emerged from the dressing room, having removed her makeup, wearing a pale grey suit and carrying a grey case, the first person she saw was Peter. He was slim and handsome with curling dark hair and deepset grey eyes, but there was an air of sadness about him and his face was pale and drawn. Then June realised with a shock that the right sleeve of his dark jacket was empty. She stopped, and as he looked up his eyes were smiling at her.

"Who taught you to sing like that?"

"Gordon Clinton."

"He did well." Peter glanced down at the case in June's hand. "I'm sorry I can't carry it for you, but ... I've lost both my arms."

"Oh, really. How interesting," said June.

Peter had been used to many reactions, but this was unique. No sympathy, no sentimentality, no "poor boy, dear, dear". She was simply – interested. It was refreshing.

At this point, the Chairman of the Entertainments Committee, who knew Peter, came out and introduced them, but Peter felt no need of an introduction. June was the most completely natural person he had ever met – whatever she felt, she said – conversation was as natural as breathing.

As they strolled down the pier and he walked with her to her digs, she chatted about her life in show business. She was so completely uninhibited, so alive and interested in everything, that he found himself talking to her as if he had known her for years. As they parted outside June's digs in Egerton Street, he asked tentatively,

"Shall I see you again?"

June's reply was typical. "Of course!"

That evening he took her to the Grand Hotel in New Brighton.

"How did you lose your arm?" she asked, as soon as they had settled in comfortable chairs in the bar.

So Peter told her, and June accepted it as naturally as she accepted the stares of the other people in the bar and the necessity to hold his drink to his lips, light his cigarette and take the money from his pocket.

To Peter she was as stimulating as a breath of sea air as she sat there drinking her orange squash.

"Don't you ever drink alcohol?" he asked with interest.

"Not since I got drunk at a party. I wasn't used to drinking and I drank gin as though it were lemonade. I was ill for a whole week, and I've never touched it since. Besides, it's bad for the complexion."

"It would be a pity to spoil yours," agreed Peter eyeing her appreciatively. "How did you first start in show business?"

"Well . . ." June threw back her head and gazed up at the ceiling of the bar. "It started when I was still at school. I'm double jointed. You know, I can bend in half backwards and put my head between my legs, or put my leg round my neck . . . Anything like that. I'll show you one day."

Peter grinned. "I can't wait." He was beginning to enjoy himself.

"One day the music teacher told my mother, 'You ought to have this child trained for dancing, she has a natural rhythm'. So she did, and I learnt tap, ballet, Greek, acrobatic, the lot.

"Then, when I was thirteen, I started singing lessons, and later we used to go out to the gun-sites entertaining the troops, a whole crowd of us in a big hall, under Miss Dolly Walsh. It was great fun. We had a meal in the officers' mess afterwards and then we would crowd into the coach and sing lustily all the way home. Another girl and I, Teresa, used to sing hymns. We were terribly holy! I once took the lead singer's place and sang two Irish songs. I was about fifteen." She turned her head and looked directly at him. "I was very shy as a child, you know."

"You shy? I can't believe it."

"Yes, I was," insisted June. "I hadn't much confidence at all. Then I took it into my head that I wasn't going to go to the gun-sites any more, I was going to concentrate mainly on religious singing. So I left them. I had piano lessons too, but I dropped them after a couple of years. I wasn't particularly good at sight reading."

"That must be rather a disadvantage for a singer," said Peter, smiling.

"It never bothered me much," said June. "Anyway I'd won this scholarship to Canterbury Art School by then, learning dressmaking and designing. That was fun, too. When I left, at seventeen, I started singing lessons with Gordon Clinton, but I decided I'd better have a trade so I went into hairdressing for three years. Mr. and Mrs. Pawsey ran the hairdressers. A very nice couple indeed. I enjoyed that."

"You didn't waste any time!"

"Oh, no, I've never wasted a minute!" June threw back her head and laughed uproariously. Several people turned round as though keen to join in the joke. Then, just as swiftly, her face became serious – all traces of laughter gone.

"I was baptised at fifteen, by total immersion. I accepted Jesus as my saviour, which has coloured my whole life since then." Her blue eyes regarded Peter thoughtfully. "Do you believe in God?"

"I'd like to," said Peter, slightly shaken by the directness of her question.

"What do you mean, you'd 'like to'?" pursued June. "I don't see how anybody can live without faith."

" I certainly believe in the teachings of Christ. I think

71

the things he said were marvellous, and that one should try to live by them..."

"I believe in it *all* – lock, stock and barrel," said June emphatically. "But that's the way I am. I can't do anything by halves. I throw myself into whatever I do... completely. And I enjoy it. I enjoy life enormously."

Peter smiled. "I can see that."

It was so evident just from looking at her. She radiated zest for life. Her blue eyes shone, her skin was radiant with health, her hair gleamed and bounced with vitality, her personality was vibrant.

June picked up Peter's glass and held it to his lips. "Why don't you drink through a straw?" she asked.

"It isn't very satisfactory. In hot drinks straws become soft and mushy and they also seem to spoil the taste of most drinks. But there we are. It's just one of those things that will never be the same..."

June put the glass firmly on the table, unaware of the glances that sidled in their direction. Sensing a trace of self-pity and cynicism in his voice, she deliberately said, "I don't feel a bit sorry for you. Do you want me to?"

"No." Peter ignored the stares, which he suddenly felt were totally unimportant. "It's quite a change to meet someone who isn't sorry for me."

"Well, I never will be. I'd like to help you though. I like helping people."

"You're helping me by being with me, by talking the way you do. I like it."

"You do?" She beamed at him. "I'm not everyone's cup of tea. I think I'm too much for them."

"You're not too much for me."

"That's good." June settled back comfortably in her chair and gazed around her.

"Tell me more about yourself. Where were you born?" asked Peter.

"Whitstable. I come from a big family. And you?"

"I was the only one."

"That's sad."

"I didn't find it sad," said Peter emphatically. "Life was pretty good till this happened."

"And then you thought you were finished." She looked at him keenly. "I don't think you're finished. I think you're just beginning."

"Beginning what?"

"A new life."

"I hope you're right."

"I know I am," said June. "I'm seldom wrong, not when I have a strong feeling about something . . . or someone."

"You're a very unusual girl."

"Yes, I know. Do you mind?"

"I like it."

"Good." June sat back with a reminiscent gleam in her eye. "There were seven of us at home. My sister Phyllis, my two step-sisters . . . my mother was Daddy's second wife . . . and the young maid. We shared everything. There were no favourites, and no question of who ruled the house either. It was Mummy. And we all got on like a house on fire – except when we fought."

"Fought?" Peter raised his eyebrows.

"Well, all families disagree sometimes. It's only natural. I suppose you had no one to fight with?"

"No."

"More's the pity."

"You have some odd ideas," said Peter.

"Have I? I think you missed a lot. Well, anyway, Whitstable is on the Thames Estuary. During the war the Nazi planes used to fly over, and they'd unload their bombs into the Estuary on their way back, if they had any left. Once Phyllis and I were sleeping on top of the Morrison Shelter when they came over, and Mummy jumped on the shelter and flung herself on top of us,

73

covering our faces. She didn't want us maimed or disfigured. The property just at the back of us was damaged, but we were all right. I was about fourteen at the time. I said to Mummy, 'It's no use worrying. If God wants me he'll take me, but if he has work for me to do here, then I'll be spared.' Well," June looked at her watch. "I'll have to get back and get my beauty sleep or I'll look like a hag in the morning."

"Impossible," said Peter.

"You can be very gallant when you want to, but I must go just the same."

"Just as you say," agreed Peter, getting reluctantly to his feet.

The lights were already switched on as they emerged into the dusk and walked along the front.

"The sea always looks more romantic at this time of night," said Peter.

"Yes," June stopped and they both gazed in silence at the darkened waves curling on to the beach under a pale moon.

"It's a lovely night," she said, turning away, and as they walked slowly towards Egerton Street, she began to sing softly to herself.

"That's nice," said Peter. "You have a beautiful voice. How long did you study under Gordon Clinton?"

"For three years, until I was twenty. I used to go in the evenings, he didn't live far from us. I liked him very much, a charming man with a very nice voice. He used to sing at concerts at the Albert Hall, and with Sir Thomas Beecham. As a matter of fact, our voices were somewhat similar in range. He was a great help to me."

She giggled. "He wasn't sure whether I was a contralto or a mezzo soprano, so they took me to the Guildhall School of Music and I saw this professor and he said it was a most unusual voice with an unusual range. I could sing 'Old Man River' like Paul Robeson and yet I could

74

get right to the top. They eventually decided I was a mezzo contralto. Well..." She stopped outside No. 12. "Goodnight, and thanks for the drink."

Peter looked up at her as she stood on the step. "When can I see you again? Tomorrow?"

"Yes, of course; but I have to rehearse in the evening. Come round after the show at five."

As Peter walked towards the bus stop he felt as though he had just emerged from a cold shower: the tingling sensation, the glow, the exhilaration, were all present. June's zest for and enjoyment of life had communicated itself to him. The following afternoon he was on the pier well before three.

"Happy Time" was a good show, compact and lively, with Joe Ring as the comedian, Gil Roberts at the piano, a soubrette called Kay Biddulph, and Len and Joyce Forum who did an instrumental act. They all joined in the comedy sketches, and June did acrobatics and sang. She thoroughly enjoyed herself, and so did the audience.

June joined Peter after the show and they walked along the front and found two deck chairs facing the sea. Peter leant back in his chair. With the warmth of the sun on his face and this charming girl beside him, he felt totally relaxed. He turned his head slowly towards her.

"What did you do after you'd finished the singing lessons?"

"I thought I'd combine singing with dancing and go on the stage. I saw Gordon Ray's name in 'The Stage', took the five a.m. workman's train to London, and they gave me a job in the chorus for three weeks at Grantham and Minehead."

"How did you like that?"

"It was the first time I'd been away from home, and I was terribly homesick. My mother was a very dominant personality and she meant everything to me, but I had a nice motherly landlady who helped a lot. When that finished I went back to London and stayed at the Theatre Girls Club in Greek Street for three weeks, waiting for work. It was a funny place." She threw back her head and chortled. "We slept in cubicles, said grace before meals, and had to clock in and out. There was a good crowd of girls there though; they used to call me Miss Naïve."

"Were you?"

June pondered. "I suppose I'd had a rather sheltered upbringing, and I wasn't very sophisticated in those days."

"Are you now?"

She grinned at him. "I don't suppose I am. Anyway I toured a number of other theatres after that. Nineteen forty-nine was a wonderful summer and we had some smashing times. That winter I was chosen to be principal girl in 'Dick Whittington' at Boston, Lincolnshire."

"Had you got over your homesickness by then?" asked Peter.

"Oh, yes! I had some most interesting digs, and all the landladies were marvellous. At one place there were three funny old ladies, one had hardly any hair. They used to bring me breakfast in bed, all beautifully laid out on a silver tray. The silver needed polishing – my mother would have been horrified – it was all a little shabby but really done in the grand old style, and every night they'd run a great big bath for me, piping hot." She looked dreamily out towards the horizon, remembering.

"And what did you do after the pantomime?" Peter prompted, fascinated by this saga, and the lively way in which it was told. June's mood and expression altered with the darting frequency of a chameleon.

"I went back to London early in 1950. Somebody gave me a note to Jackson Earle and I went for an audition. I remember he was laughing his head off because I was doing everything – acrobatic, ballet, tap, singing – and I'd forgotten to bring half the music. I stayed with Derek and Majorie, my half sister, in their flat in Finchley, 'resting' and while I was waiting for something to turn up I got this job as a ward maid in the Wellhouse Hospital, Barnet, where Majorie was a staff nurse."

"Some rest!" said Peter amused. "How did you like being a ward maid? Rather different from being an actress, wasn't it?"

"It was hard work! Eight in the morning till five every day, scrubbing out wards, the lot, but I loved it. When I went for the interview I was wearing my fur coat and all my makeup. Matron gave me one look and said, 'You don't look as if you could scrub out a ward'.

" 'I can,' I said, 'You try me. Mother brought me up to it.' So she did, and afterwards she said I was the best ward maid she'd ever had. Well, I put my heart and soul into it, as I do with everything I take on. It was a most interesting experience. I had an overall that must have been made for Tessie O'Shea. But I got on well with all the patients, the children and old people particularly. I became very attached to the long standing patients and went to great pains to look glamorous for them. One old lady had a beauty of soul which shone in her face and out of her eyes. But she had a lot of pain." June's blue eyes suddenly focused on Peter acutely. "Do you get much pain?"

"I'm seldom without it," said Peter. "In my right arm as well as my left. It's known as the phantom pain."

"How curious being able to feel a limb that isn't there."

"Yes, I suppose it is," agreed Peter. "But it's a curiosity that I could well do without." He sat upright in the deck chair and leant forward, staring at two children building a fort in the sand. But he didn't see them.

"I'd rather talk about you," he said. "What did you do next?"

"Well," said June, "I was only earning three pounds a week at the hospital, which didn't go far in London, so I found myself a job on my day off, posing for portraiture at The St. Martin's School of Art in Charing Cross Road. And in the evening I posed in the nude."

"Oh? How did you feel about that?"

June laughed. "I remember blushing all over the first time I did it, but after that everything was quite all right. Nobody made a pass at me; they just treated me as something they could draw, and that was that. It was an interesting six weeks altogether. I enjoyed every minute of it. But as that was only one evening's work a week, I also got a private job posing for some Albanian artists in Earls Court. I used to lie on a red rug in front of the fire and they made charcoal sketches of me. I got 5s an hour for that. Then I got dressed, we had a lovely supper, danced to records, and I went home.

"Then I did one whole week's work for an exam. in a sitting position and, one Saturday morning, standing. Unless you've done it, you don't realise what hard work posing is, especially standing. I started to feel faint because I wasn't used to standing still and I sort of collapsed. The teacher said, 'I've got half a commando pill you can have!' That gave me stamina and I was all right afterwards, but we had to have a bit of extra time because of the amount I'd wasted collapsing. It was quite an interesting morning."

"And what did you do in your spare time?" teased Peter.

"Oh! In my spare time I made my soubrette dresses on my sewing machine," said June, quite seriously.

A shadow fell across Peter's face and he looked up to see the deck chair attendant standing over them.

"Would you take the money out of my breast pocket," Peter requested.

As naturally as if she had been doing it all her life, June

78

took out the money, handed it to the attendant, and slipped the ticket halfway into Peter's pocket.

"In May," she said, as though there had been no interruption, "it was quite exciting. I got this telegram from Jackson Earle:

CAN YOU PLEASE REPLACE NITA VALERIE'S PARTNER IN A DOUBLE ACT AND COME TO CAMBRIDGE ON SATURDAY.

"So I had a turkish bath and a good think. I'd never done a double act before and was a bit frightened about these things. I decided, Yes, I would, and off I went the next day taking my goods and chattels.

"I saw Jackson Earle, Nita Valerie, Peggy Naylor and the rest of the cast and got the gist of the show. We had a week in Luton and then up to New Brighton to start rehearsals for 'Happy Time'."

June turned the full force of her blue eyes upon him. "How do you like the show?"

"Very much. One act in particular."

June smiled widely. "I can't guess which." Then she stood up, stretched her lovely arms above her head and gave a mighty yawn.

"I must get back. I have a rehearsal tonight. We do six different shows through the season, and two shows every day. I've got to wash my hair, too."

"Why? It looks beautiful the way it is."

June laughed. "I wash it every two days."

"When shall I see you again?"

"When do you want to?"

"Tomorrow."

"Right. You can collect me at my digs."

So he did, and nearly every day throughout the rest of July and August Peter went to New Brighton Pier to see the morning or afternoon show – and June. He amused June mightily by applauding with his feet.

"You look like a seal," she teased.

79

For several weeks Peter did not even mention June to his parents. He knew his mother was dubious about people on the stage, and in any case there seemed little point in mentioning so transitory a relationship. When the season was over in September, June would be gone and another friendship would end just like the others.

His parents thought the sudden attraction the pier seemed to have for their son a little strange, but he obviously gained pleasure from going, so they made no comment.

One day in August, however, June asked, "When are you going to take me to meet your mother?"

So it was arranged. Beatrice and Nelson thought June a delightful girl and a cheerful companion for Peter. She came once or twice to the house for a meal and that, as far as they were concerned, was that. They certainly did not take the friendship seriously.

During August, Peter visited the Government Limb Fitting Centre at Roehampton where strenuous efforts were made to fit him with an artificial right arm which would be of some use to him. There were, however, two great difficulties: one was that Peter had no actual stump for a fitment, and the other was the paralysis of the left arm, as in those days the only source of control of an artificial arm was a heavy harness around the opposite shoulder. However, they did the best they could in the circumstances, Peter went home with the arm and resolutely tried to wear it.

But he found that not only was it extremely heavy and cumbersome, it served no effective purpose, as he could not move or manipulate the arm in any way. In some cases, such as getting on and off buses, it was actually unsafe, for he was unable to hoist himself on and, because of it, no one was aware he was really armless, so instead of lending a helping hand they left him to his own devices.

In the end he came to the conclusion that, in his particular case, he was far better off without any artificial aids.

Towards the end of the season June's parents came up from Whitstable to spend a week in New Brighton. Mrs. Linnett was a straightforward, forthright personality with a firm religious faith who believed in calling a spade a spade. Exceptionally fond of jewellery, she wore two gold bracelets that jingled on one wrist and a gold watch on the other. She also liked ear rings, and usually adorned each hand with four rings, one of which had a small charm swinging from it.

Mr. Linnett, fifteen years her senior and a travelling salesman, was a mild, happy-go-lucky soul who took life as it came and seldom worried about anything. They were both friendly and chatty, and Peter got on well with them.

As the summer season drew to its close, Peter thought sorrowfully of all that he was going to lose. The advent of June had been like a comet lighting up his darkened sky. How was he going to face the darkness again? June, too, was unusually subdued.

As they strolled along the front together a week before the end of the show, Peter said, "Life is going to be very empty without you."

"Yes," said June. "I've been thinking about that. Why not come home with me?"

For a second – knowing all that such a visit would entail – Peter doubted whether he had heard correctly.

"Well, would you like that?" asked June.

"Like it!" His spirits soared upwards like a shooting star. "You know I would. But what about your parents?"

"I've told them I might be bringing you. They don't seem to mind, and it will give your mother a rest."

So, in mid-September, Peter's parents drove both of them down to the Linnetts' bungalow in Whitstable, where Peter stayed for six weeks. They went on expeditions to various parts of the country; Peter met all June's friends, and occasionally passed a congenial hour or two with Mr. Linnett down at the Wheatsheaf.

For Peter, the days passed all too swiftly. For June, they were a mixed blessing. She had gone into this with her eyes wide open, but even she had not realised quite how much there would be to do. Peter had to be washed, brushed, dressed, shaved, fed and put to bed. In the beginning Mr. Linnett did much of this and saw to his toilet arrangements, but he was no longer a young man and he had a job to do. Mrs. Linnett, though always pleasant to Peter, remained aloof from the proceedings. So gradually June took over more and more, until finally she was doing everything for him.

June had worked in a hospital and, in any case, neither of them had ever suffered from any sense of personal embarrassment – natural things came naturally to them – but to look after one individual so completely could be an exhausting business. By late October June had contracted a septic throat and jaundice, and Peter had to return home.

However, always resilient, June soon recovered her health and strength, and at the beginning of December she went to stay with the Spencers in Wallasey for a few days before leaving to join the cast of Richard Stephenson's pantomime, "Cinderella", at the Empire, Dewsbury.

Peter wrote to her regularly there, with the shoulder device strapped across his body, slowly and carefully guiding the clamp-held Biro ball point pen with rotating movements of his right shoulder. A laborious process, yet the result was flawless. It would have been impossible to guess that the letter had been written by a man without the use of his hands. Nor, despite the method, did they lack spontaneity.

June spent Christmas day with the Spencers at Grove Road, travelling down from Dewsbury by coach.

"Did you have a good trip?" asked Peter, thinking how

wonderful she looked with her sparkling eyes and cheeks like rosy apples.

"It was absolutely fantastic!" said June excitedly. "The moors were like one large undulating wedding cake. The snow was quite blinding, I had to keep my eyes closed half the time because of the glare. I wished I'd brought my sun glasses!"

She chatted enthusiastically about the show, glowing with life and vitality. Energy sprang from her in waves that lifted Peter up from the moment he saw her. But all too soon she had to be on her way again.

"I'll be up to see you soon!" he promised.

Chapter Eight

TRUE TO his word, Peter went up to Dewsbury to see June a fortnight later, travelling by train from Liverpool. Nelson drove him to the station and watched anxiously as the train drew out. It was the first time Peter had travelled such a distance completely alone, the weather conditions were appalling, anything could happen. He looked so vulnerable with the one empty sleeve and the other arm hanging uselessly at his side. But Peter was filled with excitement, bolstered up by the knowledge that in two or three hours he would be with June again.

June met him at the station and they went back to her digs for a meal. Dewsbury itself was grim, with dark satanic mills and the gutters running with grey slush, but June was on top of her form. She had a splendid landlady, Mrs. Mountain, who greeted them at the door and stayed for a little chat.

"Eee, you're a loovely lass," she said, laughing broadly at some remark of June's, and giving her a motherly hug.

"She's a good soul," said June when Mrs. Mountain had gone. "She's got a pet tortoise which she keeps in the oven in winter, and during the fuel crisis she burnt some old boots to get a fire up for our baths! We've had some good notices, Peter. Listen to this:

'Richard Stephenson's "Cinderella" has set a standard which is far and away above any previous production seen at the Empire. It is not surprising that parties are coming from miles around to see a pantomime with so many excellent features.' "

"Good!" said Peter, "What does it say about you?"

" 'Prince Charming receives some excellent support from June Lynette as Dandini.' " She grinned at him. "Come and have some food. You must be starving."

Mrs. Mountain had cooked them a meal with a superb Yorkshire pudding which was served as a separate course.

When later they went for a walk, the setting sun had transformed the town, suffusing the sky with dusky orange, casting dim golden shadows across the snow and softening the harsh outlines of the buildings.

"Nothing but partings," Peter said sadly that evening as they stood shivering on the platform waiting for the train to take him back to Liverpool. "But I'll be coming up again as soon as possible."

Peter made the journey to Dewsbury three times while June was at the Empire Theatre. When the pantomime closed at the end of March, June was put in touch with Ernest Page, an agent, and she went down to London to see him.

She wrote to Peter:

"Everyone at the Congregational Church in·Dewsbury was absolutely wonderful to me, and on Sunday I sang, 'O, for the Wings of a Dove' with the choir. Apparently Mr. Stephenson was so impressed that he has offered me the part of principal boy in his pantomime next year. But I haven't taken it up yet as I wanted to see Mr. Page before I decided.

He tells me that Ralph Reader, the producer of the National Light Opera Company, is looking for a replacement for Linda Hagen who's leaving to get married. The Company tours the country doing three shows, 'The Lilac Domino', 'Merrie England', and 'Chu

85

Chin Chow', and he's promised to coach me in the three parts every day for the next two weeks so that I can go for an audition. I've never done anything like this before, so I'm really raw, but I'm learning all the parts by heart.

It would be lovely to see you . . ."

So, early in April 1951, Peter and his pals, Ken Campbell, Derek Whitely and Les Laycock arrived in London in high spirits, ready to paint the town red. Peter had some business to conduct with the Air Ministry, but once that was finished he was ready to enjoy himself. June's sister, Phyllis, an attractive blonde working as a model at Dickens & Jones, joined them and together they went to the theatre and the cinema and out to splendid meals. Peter also took June dancing. He could raise his left arm just sufficiently to go round her waist, and as June was a born dancer she followed him without effort, fitting her steps naturally into his.

One afternoon they went to the Odeon, Leicester Square to see "The Mudlark". It was a film neither of them would ever forget. As the programme drew to its close, Peter turned towards June and said softly, "I love you." Then as if afraid she might not have heard him, he said it again, "I love you."

But how could June have missed that first confession of love; these were the very words she had been longing to hear. Until that moment, Peter had always behaved as if they were simply good friends. It was his belief that a man should not disclose his feelings unless he was in a position to give more than he received. But the words had come out involuntarily. He could hide his love no longer.

"And I love you," June whispered.

They emerged from the dark of the cinema bemused

and excited, and the others, seeing their happy faces, smiled at one another but made no comment.

All too soon the week was over and Peter had to return to Cheshire, leaving June behind.

So followed seven months of brief ecstatic meetings and sorrowful partings. June passed her audition and became a member of Ralph Reader's National Light Opera Company, appearing for the first time in "The Lilac Domino" at Streatham Hill Theatre on May 7th. She played the part of Madame Delcasse, looking very distinguished as an upright, grey haired French woman in her fifties, and the following two weeks was in Leeds as Ali Baba's hag of a wife, Mabubah.

During June, the company moved to Blackpool and played at the Grand. Unable to bear the extended parting, Peter made plans to stay at the BLESMA Home for a week to be near her. They went out together during the day and in the evening he watched June in his and her favourite part, Jill-all-alone in "Merrie England". Here she showed her true versatility by appearing as a fey young creature of the woods. In a tattered dress with long hair streaming, she looked like an untamed nymph and sang like an angel.

It was wonderful to have a whole week together, but it passed so quickly. June had become very precious to Peter, but he did not feel he had the right to put his longing into words. He could never ask her to share his life – a crippled life in which so much of the burden would fall on her.

One day they were sitting on the couch in June's digs, drinking coffee, when June said, "You're looking very thoughtful. What are you thinking?"

"I was thinking that I can no longer visualise a life without you. But I shall have to."

"Why?"

He looked up from his cup. "You know why. I have so little to offer you."

"I think you've got everything. You love me, don't you?"

"You know I do."

"And I love you. We're happy together and miserable apart. Why *be* apart?"

"You mean . . . you would marry me?" he asked in disbelief, "knowing everything that's entailed?"

"Of course I would. I was *sent* to marry and look after you. I have always known that. Our paths were destined to cross."

"I think I'm the most fortunate man alive," Peter said in all sincerity.

Later, they went for a walk. Peter will always remember the way June tucked her arm through his and, for a moment, rested her head on his shoulder. His step was buoyant. He knew, now, what it meant to be walking on air. It was the happiest day of his life. Now, indeed, he could "count his blessings"!

Two days later Peter had to return to Wallasey and June went on with the company to Bradford. Peter wrote to June:

"Last night I told my folks the glad news and they took it just as I told you they would – quietly but obviously thrilled. They'll help us as much as they can I'm sure. We talked for some time over things and they are looking forward to seeing you. This is the most marvellous thing that has happened to me – that you should want to marry me in spite of everything. Sometimes I wonder if it's really true . . . !"

Towards the end of the month June had a holiday, with no more shows for six whole weeks. She went home first and announced to her parents that she was planning to marry Peter. Her mother was horrified. Though she liked

Peter personally, she had no desire to see her daughter tied to a man without arms for the rest of her life. June was an idealist, but she was also practical. Mrs. Linnett tried to appeal to her practical side.

"How is he going to look after you financially when he's only got his disability pension?"

"There's his elocution practice," said June, "and I shall go on working."

"What! For the rest of your life?"

"Why not? I love the stage. I'd be lost without it. Peter would never ask me to give it up, knowing what it means to me."

"I don't expect he would."

"When I become famous, then he can share in my triumphs, and have a good life through me."

"You'll have to look after him, do everything for him, for the rest of your life," Mrs. Linnett reminded her daughter. "What time will you have left to become famous?"

"Peter's mother will look after him when I'm away, just as she has always done."

"She's not getting any younger."

"Oh!" exclaimed June with impatience. "You throw up so many obstacles."

"I'm not inventing them, they're *there*."

Mr. Linnett said very little, but June knew that he, too, was unhappy about the situation and worried on her behalf.

For the first time, June wavered. She journeyed up to Wallasey with a heavy heart. She hated crossing swords with her parents, and knew that much of what they said was true. But she also still believed that this was the role that she had been destined to play: the most important role of all.

The day after June arrived at Grove Road, she and

Peter sat on the sandhills of Harrison Park looking out across the sea, and had a serious discussion.

"You know what I feel," said Peter, "but I mustn't attempt to persuade you. It wouldn't be right. You must make your own decision."

"I have made my decision."

"And now you're wondering whether it is the right one."

"I hate disagreeing with my parents. They've never interfered before. They must feel very strongly about it."

"Yes. I can understand how they feel," said Peter, "but you can assure them that my sole aim in life will be to make you happy, and I will do anything and give my last penny to achieve that aim."

"I know, darling." There was an unusual tenderness in June's voice; then she stood up abruptly and threw her arms above her head. "Now let's forget about it. We've got three whole weeks in which to have fun!"

Those weeks flew by, and once again Peter went to the station to see June off on the train.

"Three wonderful weeks together," he wrote that evening, "and now we are hundreds of miles apart. I miss you already, but I hope that everything is going smoothly at home. Give my love to your folks. Optimism is the key word! As long as we keep our faith and understanding in one another, there is no reason why we shouldn't be very happy . . ."

The following day he wrote again:

"Just a short note to say Ken and I are coming to London and staying at Aunt Hilda's. I will be pleased to meet your folks and try and make them understand that although we realise that there *are* snags, we are so well suited to one another and, what is more important, in love with one another, that our marriage will be a happy one. I have enough money to make a

90

home for you, and my pension, although not huge, is a regular income, which is augmented by my 'school' and your stage work, which is not being interrupted. My parents, as you know, will help all they can . . ."

Mr. and Mrs. Linnett met Peter in London for a chat. It soon became obvious that June's father had accepted the situation. He finished by wishing them both the best of luck, and offering to help them out with furniture and bedding through Rylands, the firm where he was employed, as June and Peter were already making excited plans for redecorating and furnishing three rooms in Grove Road where they were to make their first home. Mrs. Linnett made no comment on the situation; she had "washed her hands of the whole affair".

For three weeks in August, June was playing at Butlin's Theatre, Skegness, and Campbell McCrae drove Peter there for a weekend.

Peter wrote to June on his return to Wallasey:

"It was lovely seeing you, but it went so swiftly. I hadn't got used to the idea of being with you before I had to go. As Mac said in his solemn way, 'They are not exactly ideal conditions in which to carry on a courtship!'"

When, early in October, the National Light Opera Company played for a week at the Winter Gardens, Morecambe, Peter was driven up by his parents and stayed there for three blissful days, during which time he and June became officially engaged. Peter presented June with an engagement ring which he had had specially made for her, and June gave him an electric razor specially inscribed. June says that if electric razors had not been invented, she would never have married him. Peter counters that if they had had to rely on a cut-throat, he would never have married her!

91

Then Peter had to return to Wallasey. But Albert Marrion drove him back to Morecambe in time to see June again in her last evening show there. Marrion, Wallasey's leading photographer, had become a very good friend to Peter. A tall, fluent, enigmatic man with a domed forehead and confident bearing, he found Peter photogenic, took a number of photos of him, and had several enlargements prominently displayed in his window.

Marrion, or Rion as he was called by all his friends, took Peter out and about a good deal during the year 1951, but the first time he met June was in her dressing room at the Winter Gardens Theatre.

"Gay, bright and happy, a very attractive personality, with much to give," he thought her "absolutely right for Peter. There was never a dull moment between them when they were together."

On the Sunday the three of them returned to Wallasey and Rion threw a little party in his flat and included Ken Campbell and Phyllis, June's sister, who had come to Liverpool to work as a fashion model and was now always known as Lyn.

At the beginning of November the banns were called at St. Nicholas Church, Wallasey. June and Peter had decided to spend their honeymoon at Stratford-on-Avon, and Peter had consulted Rion about this. It had to be arranged with tact as some hotels were not entirely happy about having a disabled man amongst their guests who had to be fed at the table.

Rion was friendly with the manageress of the Swan's Nest at Stratford, a Mrs. Clemens, as he was in the habit of staying at the hotel during the Shakespeare Festival, so he drove Peter down to see her one dark November day. She was a little hesitant at first, uncertain as to how her directors would greet the idea and afraid of over-stepping her authority. However, Peter's personality, good looks and charm wove their spell, and she came to the conclusion that no one could really be offended at sharing the hotel with a man who had lost the use of both arms while fighting their war, so after lunch she told Peter that he could have the bridal suite.

Mrs. Clemens did, some time later, ask if they would mind having their meals in their own room, but June stepped in with a firm "No". They would come down for meals and she would feed Peter at the table.

The National Light Opera Company completed its tour at Manchester during November, and shortly afterwards June arrived at Grove Road, filled with energy and enthusiasm, to make their three rooms look shipshape and beautiful in readiness for the reception they were planning to hold after the honeymoon.

Peter and June were married by the Reverend W. Simpson on December 12th, 1951, at St. Nicholas' Church, Wallasey, just seventeen months after they had first met. It was a quiet wedding with seven guests and a small reception afterwards at Grove Road, as Peter was anxious to avoid undesirable publicity. Their parents were there, together with Lyn and Ken, who was the best man, and Rion, who went to great lengths to see that everything went off successfully.

As June walked up the aisle on her father's arm, she thought of all that had been said in opposition to this marriage. Would they prove to be right? How could they be, when this was her destiny?

"Dearly beloved, we are gathered together here in the sight of God . . ." The well-known words washed over her as her mind flashed back to all that had happened in the past seventeen months, culminating in this day which was to change her life so radically.

In a firm, clear voice she repeated the time worn but still beautiful words which, to those listening, seemed to take on a special significance.

"I, June Graham, take thee, Peter Nelson, to be my wedded husband, to have and to hold from this day forward, for better for worse, for richer for poorer, in sickness and in health, to love, cherish and to obey, till death us do part, according to God's holy ordinance; and thereto I give thee my troth."

The minister held the ring for Peter to kiss, then slipped it on to June's finger.

After the wedding they all went back to Grove Road and enjoyed a bottle of champagne which Peter had brought back from France during the war, and kept ever since for a special occasion, "And what more special occasion could there be than this?" said Peter. Then farewells were said, Rion drove them to Lime Street Station and, with a sigh of relief that all had gone so well, he watched them depart into the winter afternoon.

The hotel in Stratford-upon-Avon was delightful, with a glowing fire to greet them in their bedroom. June carefully brushed the confetti from their clothes and the cases and they went down to the cocktail bar with all the insouciance of old hands, but their savoir faire was turned upside down when June pulled a handkerchief from Peter's breast pocket and a shower of confetti sprayed the room. Everyone else found this as funny as they did, however; the ice was broken from that moment, and they soon became good friends with all the other guests they met.

It was a perfect week. They talked, made love, walked beside the river Avon, or wandered down to the Dirty Duck, habitat of the theatrical types, and at the Swan's Nest, they filled themselves with the best food that a post-war menu could provide.

Two days after their return to Wallasey, Peter and June held a reception at Grove Road to which sixty of their friends and relatives were invited to meet them as man and wife. June enjoyed being a housewife and experimenting with new recipes for her husband and they were ideally happy in their little flat.

Now, Peter felt he had an aim and purpose which lent an urgency to living that had been lacking before. Now he had something to work for. He loved his wife and he wanted to give her the world. What had he to offer? A broken body, a humble pension, and an insignificant job teaching children how to "speak proper". If June had taken a great deal on trust, so had Peter. Trust in himself. How was he going to achieve that aim?

Chapter Nine

LESS THAN a month after their wedding, June was off again, joining the National Light Opera Company in London to rehearse for the coming season. Peter felt as though he had been torn apart. It was too painfully soon! On January 7th he wrote:

> "When the train jerked out of the station taking you with it, I think it was the saddest moment of my life, and when I went to bed last night I felt desolate, yet your presence was everywhere in the room. As you once said, husband and wife should be together, especially when they love each other as much as we do."

June was equally unhappy. She pined for Peter and found it increasingly difficult to project herself into the parts she was supposed to be playing. It all seemed meaningless. What was the point of being married if they were to be kept apart like this?

On January 21st, June was told by the producer that she would no longer be needed by the Company as she was "not worldly enough' 'for the part of Louise Panache in "The Lisbon Story". She did not know whether to rejoice or weep. It would be so wonderful to be back home with Peter again, where she felt she belonged, and yet she had wanted to make a success of this venture; it was part of their agreement that she should continue with her career. She was torn both ways.

More gadgets: *right*, a specially adapted telephone and, *below*, Peter's method of writing with the pen in his mouth.

Photo by Alan Spedding

One of Peter's paintings for the Mouth & Foot Artists Association, Clare Bridge, Cambridge.

Peter, too, was overjoyed, but sad for her, and indignant. What right had they!

"I think the N.L.O.C. have treated you very badly," he wrote. "But don't worry, darling, when you come home I'll comfort you, protect you, and all your worries will disappear. When two people can make each other as happy as we do, money is secondary. Our aim must be 'happiness together': for you to have the bright lights and applause, and for me to feel I'm doing something useful and worthwhile."

Peter made several constructive suggestions as to what June might be able to do as an alternative, and finished his letter:

"With regard to your future plans, as long as what you do brings you happiness, and I'm with you, then that's all right with me."

In the end, June accepted an offer to appear for the summer season on New Brighton Pier in a new show called "Holiday Time".

Before this, however, Peter took her for a ten day holiday to Holland. Although they did not know it, this was to be the first of their many trips abroad. They stayed with Mr. and Mrs. Thiel, a charming couple who, with their son, Marius, now abroad, had given hospitality to Peter when he was visiting the country with his school at the age of thirteen. Once having made contact with friends overseas, Peter always liked to keep in touch, and later on there were many with whom he corresponded regularly. It gave him pleasure both to give and to receive hospitality.

June enjoyed playing in "Holiday Time" even more than in 1950, for not only was it a happy show, but it meant that she could be with Peter for the whole of the summer, which was what she really desired.

The greatest gift which June brought to their marriage was to treat Peter like a man, no different in any respect from other men. She was not gentle with him, she was tough. She dared him to attempt things which at one time he might have considered beyond him. She encouraged him to do everything possible for himself: to *live* his life. Diametric opposites, flint against stone, they drew the best out of each other. June was the spur, but Peter was her reason for living. There was never anything half-hearted about her. With an excess of vitality she would burst into song, filled with the joy of living. Her laughter was boisterous and rang often through those upstairs rooms at Grove Road.

She had exploded into Peter's world with all the force and fire and colour of a comet. Not every man would have had the strength to take her on – fearing to be swamped by her, to drown in all this exuberance. But Peter was June's rock. She threw herself up against him in all her moods, and bounced right back again. In an ever-changing world he could be relied upon not to change. He was the anchor she needed, or she might destroy herself trying to find her identity. Which, out of all these people, was she? For there was not one June but a dozen, all in the space of an hour: quiet, reflective, vivid, gay, or sunk in bottomless silence. Moody, waspish, ingenuous and kind, she could be an angel, or act like an obstinate child. Totally honest and not abounding in tact, she said whatever came into her head, making no attempt to repress her feelings.

She could twist the knife; but Peter, too, had an underlying toughness. Not particularly sensitive, and with a remarkable capacity for ignoring that which he did not wish to absorb, he never stopped loving June because of the good feeling that glowed from her. If she was angry she shouted, but when she was happy she was bouncing, dancing, shining with it like the limelight which she so much enjoyed on the stage.

It was during 1952 that fate stepped in with one of those coincidences which had occurred more than once in Peter's life. He came across a "Believe it or Not" item in a magazine which described the incredible achievements of a German whose name, Erich Stegmann, did not mean anything to Peter at that time. This man had been attacked by polio at the age of three and lost the use of both hands and arms. His legs were also affected, but from the first he was a fighter. He insisted on being accepted as a perfectly normal child, he went to an ordinary school and, despite his drawbacks, excelled there, particularly in painting, which he did from the beginning with the brush held in his mouth, as the illustration showed. Now in his thirties, Stegmann was a brilliant and prolific painter who had won many awards and supported himself more than adequately by his work.

"Well, if he can do it, why can't I?" thought Peter. "All I need are the materials . . ."

It was just two days later that Miss Edith Walker, a friend of Beatrice Spencer's, to whom she had given solace and help both before and after her sister Adelaide's recent death, said, "Adelaide left some oil paints and canvases. I wonder if they would be of any use to Peter?"

Beatrice accepted them gladly, and the following day Peter picked up a paintbrush for the first time since he had left school. Looking once again at the photograph of Stegmann, he clamped the brush firmly between his teeth, dipped it into some paint which his mother had squeezed on to the palette, mixed it carefully, and, with the canvas laid flat on the table in front of him, proceeded to paint a vase of flowers.

Peter had never thought of himself as artistic, and had done the minimum of painting at school, but this in no

99

way deterred him. Now was his chance! He did the painting completely from memory, in the way he imagined flowers to be. There were lupins, sweet williams and a large red and yellow flower. He wasn't quite sure what this was supposed to represent, but when he had finished, it reminded him more of a gas jet blazing out of the centre. The perspective was somewhat odd, but at least it was eye-catching, and not too bad, he thought, for a first effort. It took him a long time, of course, but then he had plenty of that at his disposal.

As soon as he had finished this, Peter started another painting; a copy of a postcard, with trees and sky and a few houses. He was slightly more pleased with this one; the perspective was better, the trees and houses looked reasonably true to life, and it had a continental air about it. Edith Walker was delighted at this turn of events, for she was convinced that Adelaide was looking down on Peter and guiding his brush.

Initially Peter painted with the brush held in his front teeth, but later he found that to grip it firmly with the back teeth gave him more control over the brush. At first it was just a pleasant way of passing the time, but at the back of his mind lay the thought that, perhaps one day, something more would come of it. So Peter fitted in his painting between the elocution lessons. It was a release from some of the inevitable frustrations of his life, it gave him pleasure, and was one of the few creative outlets left to him. He was now in the happy position of being able to give something of his own making to others, and he presented one of his paintings to Miss Walker, and another to Campbell and Mary McCrae on the eve of their wedding.

Peter did not know it, but this was the beginning of a whole new life which was to open up before him like a jewel box.

At the end of September the New Brighton Pier show

finished, and June had a holiday in Swalecliffe with her parents to recharge her batteries. She had used up a good deal of nervous and physical energy throughout the year, and found the change, rest and relaxation sent her back to Peter refreshed in mind and body.

In October June returned to Grove Road to pursue her calling as extra-ordinary housewife. She had several club dates throughout 1952 and 1953, and also sang in the Church choir and occasionally with the B.B.C., but there was not, at this stage, a great demand for her type of singing. Ballads were on their way out and rock and roll was swamping the stage and television screen.

Early in 1953 Peter had his first actual illness for many years. Being the possessor of a strong constitution, and an equable temperament not given to worry concerning either the past or the future, he was rarely if ever ill in the accepted sense. Nor did he suffer from minor ailments such as colds which could, in his case, have been a major problem.

Peter had planned to take June to a dance, but when the day arrived he was not feeling at all well, and the pains in his legs made him suspect flu. As he had already bought the tickets and did not want to disappoint June, Peter asked Rion if he would like to go in his place.

While June was away, however, Peter was violently sick and began to have acute pains in his stomach. He was ill during the night and, at dawn, June rang the doctor who diagnosed appendicitis (they later discovered he had peritonitis) and immediately phoned for an ambulance. The ambulance men arrived complete with stretcher.

"Good heavens," said Peter. "I don't need a stretcher!"

But the attendants would have none of this and Peter was duly carried into the ambulance. He arrived in hospital at eight a.m. on the Saturday, the operation was completely successful, they took out the stitches at the end of a week and sent him straight home. June was shocked by his appearance. The overworked nursing staff had little time to devote to his special needs, his hair was unkempt, and he looked considerably neglected. But once home again and under June's vigilant eye, he soon recovered his old resilience and looked spruce and well cared for.

Shortly afterwards, Florence Nesmith wrote to Peter telling him that she and her husband were planning a trip to Britain, where they hoped to meet some of the fifteen hundred R.A.F. cadets to whom they and their American friends had given hospitality in Florida during the war. The Nesmiths were regaled in London, Scotland, Wales and Ireland and arrived in Liverpool in mid-June. Peter and another ex-cadet, Ken Gedling, made exhaustive efforts to gather together all the Merseyside pilots who at one time had been entertained by Florence and Ira Nesmith. The party at the Adelphi Hotel, during which they were presented with an engraved silver tray, was a great success, with about fifty of the "boys" and their wives attending.

"Although I've lost touch with many of the boys who visited our home, nearly all the fifteen hundred send me Christmas cards each year," said Mrs. Nesmith in her speech of thanks. "We have been planning to see our boys again for a long time and are delighted that it has coincided with Coronation year.

"But it still came as something of a surprise to see how most of you have changed. The slim boys in their late teens are now grown men in their thirties. In most cases, something new has been added – wives and, for many, children. I even had to ask some of you who you were," she said a little sadly, "despite the fact that I had probably just received letters from you. But it is wonderful to be with you all again and we shall remember this trip with deep pleasure for the rest of our lives."

Mrs. Nesmith had remembered Peter with warmth and affection, and they had corresponded regularly two or three times a year. Although she was shocked to see what the war had done to him, she was filled with admiration for his achievements, and for his lovely wife. In fact, in many ways he seemed to her less changed than some of the other boys with whom she renewed acquaintance.

In August of that year June had two weeks holiday with her parents, and Peter, with Rion and Ken Campbell, spent the Bank holiday weekend in Aberdaron, a small but popular village on the coast of North Wales, where a new experience awaited him. It was magnificent weather and on the Saturday Rion suggested they all went for a swim.

"Fine!" said Peter. "I'll come and paddle at the edge."

Rion and Ken swam to a rock about twenty yards out, leaving Judy, Rion's Boxer bitch, on the shore. Peter stood at the edge watching them, with Judy crying and whining beside him. She hated being left behind but she had never braved the sea before. Suddenly, distraught at being left out of things, she took the plunge, and swam out victoriously to join her master.

Well, why not? thought Peter. Why be left out? And walking into the sea up to his thighs, he hopefully pushed his feet off the sea bed and let himself fall through space on to his back. It was a frightening moment as his head went under and he floundered helplessly, wondering if he would ever regain his balance without arms to support him, but he kept cool and in another second he was lying flat on top of the water, floating. It was the most exhilarating experience he had enjoyed for a long time. Here was something else he could do! He need not just sit back and watch the others. He could be one of them. Exultantly he kicked out his legs and shot backwards, delighted to find he could work up quite a speed.

"Hey!" shouted Ken in horror. "What are you doing? You'll drown!"

"No, I won't," said Peter. "You watch me!" and steering himself round, he kicked out passionately and went on kicking the twenty yards to the rock, where he gleefully joined them.

"That's pretty marvellous," said Rion. "How do you feel?"

"Never felt better," puffed Peter. "It's the Channel for me tomorrow!"

From that day onwards Peter never lost an excuse to swim, both in the sea and in the swimming baths at home.

At first he had been inclined to keep his shoulders covered to hide from the public the scarred amputation, the thin left arm and the wasted back muscles, not for his sake but for theirs – feeling it was not a pretty sight for others. But then he came to the conclusion that the public should be educated to accept such sights and mix with the disabled normally instead of segregating them.

Later in the month he went for a week's holiday with Rion to Combe Martin, North Devon, where he swam as often as possible.

Rion had booked a double room with twin beds and a private bathroom, as Peter had to be looked after. It was a delightful hotel perched on a rock with a blaze of flowers in the garden. When they reached their room Rion took off his jacket and proceeded to unpack. He looked up from his case with a shirt in his hands and saw Peter standing there, smiling at him. It suddenly dawned that Peter was quite incapable of doing any of these things. Everything would have to be done for him.

"Sorry!" he said. "I forgot!" He took off Peter's jacket and hung it up, unpacked his case and put the things away, gave Peter a wash and combed his hair.

"Lucky you don't need a shave!" he said wryly, and started on his own chores, thinking, It's going to be quite an unusual holiday. For this was the first time Rion had been completely in charge, as previously Ken Campbell had done what was necessary.

They went downstairs for a meal and Rion held Peter's glass to his lips, cut up his food and fed it to him mouthful by mouthful. In between, he dealt with his own meal. Suddenly he groaned.

"Anything wrong?" asked Peter.

"I must have a rest. My arm's aching."

Peter smiled at him. "You have your rest. It takes getting used to, doesn't it?"

After a day or two Rion settled into the routine and, together with Judy, Rion's Boxer, they toured the Devonshire countryside, making friends wherever they went. There was one day, however, which stood out in Rion's memory as being distinctly less happy than the rest. They decided to go home via Lynmouth and Minehead, and were going down Porlock Hill, a particularly steep gradient, when Rion realised that the brakes had become overheated and they were not going to hold the car. For a moment he said nothing, hoping that they would be able to make it. He had put the car into low gear, the brakes were hard on but seemed entirely ineffective. The heavy car was gaining speed. He was terribly conscious of Peter sitting beside him, helpless, without arms to break the impact or protect himself in any way. He had to warn him.

"Peter, I don't think we're going to make it. The car is out of control."

Peter sat there quite calmly, accepting what came, well aware there was nothing he could do to prevent it.

"We're going to career down the hill at a hell of a speed. Hold everything." Rion said tensely.

What with? Peter thought, with automatic irony.

He lowered his head, pushed his feet out in front of him and hoped for the best.

"I'm going to turn into that lay-by and head for the

trees," Rion muttered. "It's the only thing that will stop us."

They hit the tree with force, the impact jarring them both and throwing Judy off the back seat.

"God!" exclaimed Rion. "I was afraid your head would go through the windscreen." He regarded Peter with a worried face. "Are you all right?"

Peter reassured him. "I'm fine, but what about the car?"

Rion opened both doors and they got out and surveyed the damage.

"Well, the bumper's a write off," said Rion, "and the left wing looks a mess. Let's hope there's no internal damage. I'll go and find a phone box and get a breakdown van."

"I'll come with you," said Peter.

Rion looked at him with respect. "You didn't turn a hair."

Peter shrugged. "It wouldn't have been much use, would it? We were lucky there was gravel on the lay-by to help slow us up."

"We were lucky altogether."

The car was repaired the same day and within a few hours they were on their way again, both of them having brushed the incident from their minds.

"Inadvisable to mention it at home though," said Rion as they drove through more manageable terrain. "It might upset your family." Peter fully concurred. There was no sense in putting a blight on what had been an exceptionally pleasant holiday.

In October of that year Peter sat down at his desk and penned a letter to the *Daily Express*. There had recently appeared in the press a good deal of controversy about the Commonwealth Air Force Memorial at Runnymede which had cost £140,000 to build, and Peter decided to add his comment.

"Dear Sir,

I was one of the 'sons who went forth into the dangerous unfamiliar sky and helped to save the world.' I came back from the war having lost both my arms and am writing this with a gadget attached to my shoulder.

Would it not be better to spend such amounts of money to assist the disabled, who have to go on living?

The dead will always be remembered by their loved ones, no matter how many war memorials are built."

Peter was very startled at the response this called forth. Letters started arriving by every post; from the disabled, from parents whose sons had been killed in that same war, from old age pensioners. In all, he received nearly forty letters, and all of the writers without exception expressed sympathy with Peter's sentiments. Two or three even enclosed donations of money, which Peter found rather embarrassing, as he was certainly not asking for alms for himself but simply suggesting that the money might be better spent in more practical ways.

He was thinking in terms of a BLESMA Home, of which there were then only two in existence, one at Blackpool where he had once stayed and one at Southsea. The money for these had to be raised entirely by voluntary subscriptions, accumulated slowly over a long period by various appeals. It seemed to Peter ironic that while the public subscribed to so useful a purpose, all the government could rise to was a useless piece of masonry, which would be unveiled with ceremony and enormous publicity, and then by most forgotten.

One letter Peter received was from a Miss Rita Petley, a charming and rather lonely elderly spinster who had lost a leg in a road accident. They became good friends and he and June often met her when on one of their trips to London during the years that followed.

One of the most poignant letters, however, came from

a Mr. and Mrs. Frederick Hooper of Manchester, who wrote:

"Our son, a Pilot Officer, lost his life on flying operations and his name figures on the magnificent Runnymede Memorial, but we who have lost in the war do not need these imposing masses of stone and marble to remember our boys, and most of us feel that the monies could have been better spent in aid for the blind and maimed.

Our method of encouragement to those war-bereaved like ourselves is writing them letters to help them to live in the heritage of courage and zest for life left by their sons. Since our boy was killed in 1945 we have written over seven thousand such letters and made some wonderful friendships. We are not going to send you our pity for your incapacitation, but our deep admiration for your courage and adaptability."

Peter answered all the letters personally, some of the disabled he was able to help, and several of the letters resulted in life-long friendships.

Although Peter and June were very happy in their three upstairs rooms at Grove Road, there were certain disadvantages. The small bedroom which they had turned into a kitchenette, had no running water, so June had to carry all the water from the bathroom. At first she had washed up in the bathroom, but abandoned that after breaking too many dishes banging them against the porcelain basin.

So, early in 1954, they decided it was time they had a home of their own, and shortly afterwards Peter came across a plot of land suitable for building. The plot was too large for his requirements, but he approached the builders who agreed to let him have half the land on which they would build a small bungalow. Then came the obstacles.

First, Peter had to gain the approval of the Planning Authority. Then, he had to find the money. He had managed to save a certain amount, but this was not sufficient for the capital required, and there were snags about obtaining the mortgage through the usual channels. So Peter approached his old friend Squadron Leader Danton. Always happy to help, Danton contacted the R.A.F. Benevolent Fund, and after some considerable discussion and meetings with their representative, they agreed to lend Peter the money to be paid back over twenty-five years.

This was a source of great pleasure and satisfaction, and Peter and June together began making excited plans for their future home. Peter designed the layout of the bungalow and incorporated several features which would make life simpler for them both, including doors without locks, with rising hinges to enable them to close themselves, and magnetic catches to hold them open. The telephone, of course, had the receiver attached to the wall at ear level, the various electrical switches were at foot or shoulder level, and the front door catch was operated by foot.

Peter and June moved into the bungalow in Claremount Road in April of the following year. The removal was conducted with great efficiency. June had already made all the curtains and each piece of furniture was labelled so that the removal men knew its destiny in advance. By early evening they were so straight that they were able to invite fourteen of their friends round for housewarming drinks.

They were both delighted with their new home, and June energetically tackled the small garden. It was a wilderness when they moved in but with the help of her father and Ken Campbell, who had married her sister Lyn during the previous year, June soon had it tamed.

She had never really stopped singing, although she performed less frequently, mainly at concerts and dinners, as well as charity shows which Peter helped organise for BLESMA. During 1955 she broadcast on the Northern Home Service in a programme entitled "What Makes a Star". "I definitely think June Lynette has the makings of a star," said Flotsam (B. C. Hilliam), one of the panel. "Many top singers of today would be jealous of her range."

Meanwhile, Peter was filling in his spare moments by reading to the blind at Leeds House in New Brighton. He went regularly and read the daily newspaper to them, turning the pages with his mouth or toes. They loved hearing items concerning the royal family, or a "good murder case", items which were not normally reported on the B.B.C. news. And eventually Peter arranged a rota so that someone went there every day.

It was during this year that Peter decided to teach himself to type. He had already abandoned the awkward shoulder attachment and taught himself to write with the pen held in the mouth, but now he had more ambitious plans. He typed his first letter to June while she was staying with her step-sister, Marjorie, in London.

". . . What do you think of my typing? The machine is a small Imperial portable. It came yesterday and I am typing this with my big toe. The trouble is that my big toe is too big! And sometimes I hit two keys at once. A special attachment is to be made to fit on my shoe, which will make it easier. The paper will be supplied from a stack of what is called continuous stationery . . . I miss you darling and I am looking forward to the weekend and to hearing all the news then . . . These few paragraphs have taken me half an hour to write."

But Peter increased his speed rapidly once he had obtained the special half shoe, until eventually he was actually typing at the rate of thirty-five words a minute and could deal with all his own correspondence unaided. The typewriter was situated on the floor and he would type with his right foot, which he slipped into a half shoe fitted with a rubber "finger". His left foot he used for the shift key.

Early in 1956 Mrs. Nesmith sent Peter a card painted by Earl Bailly, a talented Canadian artist who painted brilliant pictures of the Nova Scotia land and seascape. Stricken by polio at the age of two and paralysed in both legs and arms, he had painted with the brush held in his mouth from the age of fourteen.

This set Peter thinking, and when later in the year he saw other cards painted by the same method, and published by the Association of Mouth & Foot Painting Artists, he said to June, "I think I'll have a go myself".

"Good idea!" agreed June.

So Peter wrote to the Association, asking whether they would be interested in seeing some of his paintings, and giving a few brief details about himself. When he received a reply in the affirmative he despatched half a dozen paintings. Then he sat back and waited.

Chapter Ten

THE DAYS went by and Peter began to wonder whether
the paintings had ever reached their destination. Then
one day he received a letter from the Association.

"Thank you for sending us samples of your work, but
we regret that your paintings do not come up to the
standard we require for publication."

Well that, thought Peter, is the end of that.
But he was wrong.

In May 1957 the Association of Mouth & Foot Painting
Artists wrote to Peter inviting him to an exhibition they
were holding at the Tea Centre in Regent Street, London.
He went with June and took some further canvases with
him for, despite the rebuff, he had not stopped painting.
The exhibition was an eye opener. The standard of the
paintings generally was extremely high and no one would
have realised that they had not been painted by what is
considered the normal method.

The exhibition, the first to be held in Britain, was
opened by Group Captain Leonard Cheshire, V.C., the
famous airman who was British Observer at the dropping
of the atomic bomb in 1945. He later became a Roman
Catholic and founded the Cheshire Homes, devoting his
life to looking after the disabled and chronic sick.

One of the first artists Peter was to meet was Corry
Riet, a painter of Dutch landscapes. So gay, cheerful and

lively was she that no one would have imagined she had been paralysed since the age of five. Corry had never allowed this to quell her spirit. She had taught herself to paint with her mouth and had travelled the world in her wheelchair.

"Have you met Erich Stegmann, our president?" she asked Peter.

Peter said he had not yet had that pleasure.

"Oh!" exclaimed Corry, "he is a wonderful man, really wonderful! He is so great an artist and he has so big a heart. He changed my life, he makes it possible for us to paint and not to worry all the time about where the money is coming from to live. He is a great man, there is no one like him!"

Peter received this eulogy with restrained scepticism, but when he met Erich Stegmann and had managed to piece together his story from his conversations with other artists, he realised that what Corry had said was true. Erich Stegmann was unique. It also became clear to Peter that this was the very man who had first inspired him to paint, after reading of his artistic achievements in the "Believe it or Not" column several years previously.

A short, thickset man with a forceful jaw line and a dynamic personality, one barely noticed that Stegmann's arms were useless and that he wore a built up shoe. By a combination of talent and willpower he had carved out a successful career for himself and won numerous awards in the field of art with his powerful and arresting paintings. In 1947, at the age of thirty-four, he had decided to turn his mind and restless energies to the plight of others whose handicaps were, in many cases, even more severe than his own.

Believing that artists who painted with the mouth or foot would find it easier to market their work collectively and that, once freed from financial worry, they would be able to devote themselves to their art, he sought out disabled artists throughout the world who had previously been working in isolation.

Stegmann and his colleages eventually formed an international association with its headquarters in Liechtenstein. Since then Stegmann had travelled the world organising exhibitions and continually seeking out new artists who could be helped in this way.

As Erich Stegmann spoke only German, his conversation with Peter was held through an interpreter.

"Your work shows talent," he told Peter, "but the standard is not yet sufficiently high for us to accept your paintings for reproduction throughout the world on cards and calendars. I suggest that you attend art school and we will give you a scholarship to cover the cost of your tuition and materials."

Peter was delighted with this offer and the confidence Stegmann showed in his future abilities. He lost no time in signing on at the Wallasey School of Art, and started in the new term with high hopes. If he could succeed in this it would make a considerable difference to his life. He would be able to offer June all the things he wanted her to have, and so far had not been able to give her. But this was still only supposition.

First he had to work. And work he did. Philip H. Smith, a lecturer at the School of Art, had never had a more ardent pupil. Peter attended four times a week; he also painted at home and continued to teach elocution. His first art lesson he found rather bewildering. Philip Smith said, "Come into this room and make some sketches. Hold the pencil in your mouth and see what you can do."

Peter started to follow him in but stopped abruptly at the door. The model was stark naked. This shook him for a moment, never having been in a life class before. However, nothing daunted, he sat down before an easel, gripped the pencil bravely in his mouth, and began to draw. Philip Smith said it was reasonable for a first effort, and from there Peter went on to still life, landscape and portrait painting, attending both day and evening classes.

There was no specific course laid out for him, so he fluctuated between taking part of the courses which already existed.

Philip Smith, a first-class artist himself, was slight and fair with a pale complexion and a wide high forehead tapering down to a narrow chin. Normally more concerned with things than people, he had thought having a disabled pupil might prove a challenging problem, but very quickly found Peter was so accustomed to having to help people help him that there was no expected awkwardness or embarrassment. Although the majority of the students were in their teens or early twenties, Peter settled in quite naturally on the first day, and everyone felt completely a home with him. It seemed quite natural to hold his cup and feed him a biscuit at the tea break. He had a talent for putting people at ease.

There is, of course, a certain amount of strain on the neck muscles when painting with the mouth, so where others would use a hogs hair brush for oils, Peter preferred the softer sable brushes, and a fairly thin oily paint which would flow more easily on to the canvas. One of Peter's initial difficulties was that the brushes had a habit of getting wet and soggy after a while, and he chewed his way through dozens of them. He tried cigarette holders, polythene and bamboo. The latter seemed effective at first as it was already hollow, would hold the brush reasonably well and was not unpleasant to have in the mouth, but after a week or two it would disintegrate and Peter began to spit out splinters.

Eventually a dental surgeon friend, solved the problem by making two plastic mouth pieces which were moulded to his lower teeth, one for a fine brush and one for a thick. These held the brushes firmly with just a light pressure from the upper teeth, and proved to be most satisfactory, considerably minimising the ache in his jaws.

Philip Smith found Peter "kind, generous and helpful, with an astonishing amount of grit and guts", while his skill and dexterity at painting increased with surprising rapidity.

In the spring of 1957 Peter took June for a holiday. Captain Keith Leigh, an old school friend who had made flying his career after service in the R.A.F., rang them to say he was flying a group of Fruit Trade Importers and Exporters from Liverpool to Valencia, and there were two spare seats available which Peter could have for a very nominal sum. So Peter seized the opportunity and within twenty-four hours they were soaring across the Channel in a Dakota.

It was the first time Peter had been in a Dakota since his years as a pilot in Transport Command, and it was a rather strange experience not to be at the controls, but certainly not unpleasant, being served a good meal, with coffee and liqueurs and waited on by charming hostesses. He felt no nostalgia, and certainly no fear. He had left the old life behind him, sloughing it off like an old skin, and lived in the present. The present was good.

Valencia as a city did not equal the romantic associations of its name. Peter and June stayed there for two nights in what turned out to be a very second-class hotel where June had a bad attack of "Spanish tummy", and Keith found himself looking after Peter.

Then Peter said, "How about going on to Majorca and getting some sea and sun?"

"Marvellous!" agreed June, always game for anything. So off they went, and after six delightful days there, where they were later joined by Keith, they returned refreshed and invigorated for the work ahead.

On his return to Wallasey, Peter, who was already a member of the committee, was made Vice Chairman of the Mersey-side Branch of the British Limbless Ex-Service

Men's Association. He had also, for some time, been serving on the Disablement Advisory Committee of the Ministry of Labour, representing BLESMA. Throughout his life Peter had never turned down a request for help, and in this way he was able to assist those "who gave part of themselves in the services of their country", in particular the elderly, of whom BLESMA was mainly composed. BLESMA had fought so successfully for better conditions and increased pensions and allowances that the younger men did not feel the need for such an association, although Peter endeavoured to persuade more to join so that they might swell the numbers and aid the totally incapacitated or others less fortunate than themselves.

Peter and his colleagues spent a good deal of their time organising coffee mornings, raffles and entertainments to provide the money for cigarettes and comforts throughout the year for the members, and generous hampers at Christmas. They held a carnival dance, at which June sang in the cabaret, and in March Peter produced a charity show at the Pigalle in Liverpool with fifteen artistes including Rob Wilton, Ken Dodd and June Lynette. Rob Wilton wrote afterwards: "Good to know the show was a success, and indeed most of it due to your efforts . . ."

This was Rob Wilton's last stage appearance.

Twice Peter organised a cocktail and tombola party at the Hotel Victoria, New Brighton, with some financial backing by the local brewery. On the second occasion Peter wrote to Douglas Bader, asking if he would autograph a copy of his biography *Reach for the Sky*, so that it might be put up for auction to assist BLESMA funds. Bader replied:

"Call and see me at my office at Shell Centre, but please ring first as I'm a difficult man to get hold of, constantly flying off somewhere or other."

Peter went with June to Bader's office in London, and the legless war pilot, hero of so many famous exploits, greeted them with characteristic informality. He had the most clear sparkling, piercing blue eyes Peter had ever seen. As Bader hoisted himself up to sit on the edge of his desk, with his shirtsleeves rolled well up, Peter noticed the strong rippling muscles of his forearms, obviously the result of his using them so much to help him get about.

It was an interesting meeting, the armless pilot confronting the legless one, and they chatted for quite a while. Peter found his language a little strong considering there was a lady present – but Bader was never one to mince his words. As they parted and wished each other good luck, Bader told Peter that he was glad to see he "still had the spark in his eyes". It was a worthwhile visit, as the autographed book brought in twenty-five pounds for BLESMA's funds.

Now life really began to move forward for Peter, new events and happenings crowding in on each other in close succession.

June's sister Lyn had married Ken Campbell in 1954, and in 1957 they had their first child, Guy. June was enchanted with her small nephew and it increased the longing which she had been secretly cherishing for some time. As Peter, too, had always wanted children, they now decided that they had the accommodation and sufficient financial security to enable them to start a family. When, early in May 1958, the Association of Mouth and Foot Painting Artists invited Peter to attend their conference and exhibition in Paris, June was unable to go. She was expecting a child at the end of that month.

Peter was reluctant to leave her at such a time. However, it was only for two days and she persuaded him she would be all right since she had the family all around her. So off he went with his good friend and brother-in-law, Ken, who looked after him with his usual efficiency and absence of fuss.

They met the able young Manager of the Association's London Office and his charming wife in London, and drove to Dover, landing in Dunkirk as dawn was breaking. They then continued on to their hotel in Paris, where they met the other artists. This was a fascinating experience, and Peter was again impressed with the high standard of the paintings on exhibition.

At the dinner held for all the artists before the Annual General Meeting, Peter noticed with interest that the chairman, Erich Stegmann, who presided at the head of the table, drank his wine by gripping the glass with his teeth and tilting his head backwards.

Why not? thought Peter. It seemed an excellent idea. So he picked up the glass with his teeth but, before he had time for a sip, there was a horrifying grinding noise and the broken glass spilled its contents all across the white tablecloth. The waiters were none too pleased and Peter reflected it might have been better if he had practised first with water!

One of the most interesting people Peter met at the exhibition was Marie Louise Tovae, an auburn-haired French artist and one of the original members of the Association. With the brush held elegantly between her manicured toes, she painted in radiant colours that brought her canvases glowing to life. A friendly girl, with a warm direct simplicity which made her easy to talk to, she told Peter something about her life.

"I was born without arms, but it has not worried me too much because I have never known anything else. As a child, I learned to use my feet for the simple things of life, and for painting, which I have done since I was eighteen years old. It gives me great joy. In fact, I am always happy. People say it shows in my paintings. I think the world is a beautiful place, and I try to express some of that beauty so that others may see it too."

She smiled at Peter. "We are fortunate, you and I, to be given such a gift. Yes?"

"Fortunate indeed," said Peter. Here was a fellow soul who had learnt very early in life to "count her blessings". How his father would have approved!

Another foot painter and founder member whom Peter met at the Paris exhibition was Charles Pasche, a talented Swiss artist also born without arms who, from an early age, taught himself to paint with the brush held in the mouth. For several years he attended a famous art school in Geneva, then his father became unemployed and Pasche had to relinquish his studies and find work.

For years he lived in poverty, earning a few shillings by painting brooches and medals, or later with his wife, selling tea and coffee from door to door. Then Erich Stegmann heard of him, and Pasche joined with him in helping to form the Association of Mouth and Foot Painting Artists.

From the financial security thus gained, he was able to return to his true profession. Today, with the aid of a magnifying glass and incredible patience, he paints exquisite landscapes and flower pictures of great sensitivity and minute detail.

"In painting the beauty of flowers," he said, "I want to give back to life something which it gives to me daily."

The father of two healthy sons, he had taught himself to drive, first a bicycle, and later his own specially adapted car. He was, in fact, the first handless man to obtain an international driving licence.

Everyone Peter spoke to told a similar story, of early struggles and then of the meeting with Erich Stegmann, when their life of insecurity was changed almost over night.

Peter returned home inspired and determined to work

even harder than before. He found June in good health and high spirits. She went into Highfield Maternity Hospital several days before the baby was due, and every day Peter phoned and went to see her. Towards the end, she was in the delivery room for twenty-four hours. Peter was very worried and rang the hospital every half hour for news of her. Each time they said the same.

"No change. Nothing has happened."

Something must be wrong, he thought, and they don't want to tell me.

Then, to his great relief, at a quarter to ten in the evening they said, "Yes, I think we will have some news for you by a quarter past ten."

It was the longest half hour Peter had ever spent. When he finally heard that June had been delivered of a son and that mother and child were both doing well, his relief was unbounded. He had a son! Now his cup was truly full.

He went to see them both the following morning. June was sitting up looking very pleased with herself.

"Hello, Angel." Peter bent and kissed her. "He certainly took his time, didn't he?"

"I thought he was never coming," said June. "But it was all very interesting. Well, what do you think of our Robin? Was he worth waiting for?"

Peter looked down at the small bundle with the little red screwed up face lying in the shelter of her arms.

"He's marvellous. You both are. He looks a very determined lad. I wonder who he takes after?"

"A bit of us both!" said June. "You should have heard him cry when he was born. Nobody's going to walk over that boy!"

Later, Peter saw the doctor. "The baby's all right, is he? There's nothing wrong with him?"

"He's perfect," said the doctor emphatically. "Seven pounds, seven ounces, and a fine boy."

June came home ten days later and settled down to looking after her new baby. It was fun. Sometimes she missed the peace of the two of them being alone together in their small bungalow, but she enjoyed being a mother, just as she enjoyed being a wife. For the moment she was fulfilled.

She was also a good deal busier, and this naturally affected Peter. There simply was not the time to do everything for him as she had done in the past. So Peter began to think up ways and means of doing even more for himself.

Once Robin was old enough to sit up in a highchair and be fed, Peter realised that June could not be expected to feed three of them at once. So he fed himself. He simply bent his head and picked up the food with his mouth, "animalwise", while at the side of his plate lay a napkin on which he could wipe his mouth. Why had he not thought of it before? It was so simple, especially if the meat was cut up first, and meant he no longer had to rely on other people's whims as to what he ate and when.

Peter had also adopted two different ways of drinking unaided. He either drank from a cup by tilting it towards him, or used a plastic straw – a short one for short drinks, a long straw for the others. After a while he found that most drinks, with the exception of tea, tasted nearly as good this way: coffee, milk, alcohol, even beer. When he went down to the pub for a drink and a chat with his friends, the barman soon caught on to his requirements and would either provide a straw with his drink, or take out one of the two which protruded from his breast pocket.

During 1959 Peter's life of action really got into full swing. For nearly two years he had worked hard at art school and, under Philip Smith's guidance, his skill and draughtsmanship had improved enormously. He turned out paintings by the score: portraits, still life and landscapes. He was not interested in modern art or abstract painting, but liked to paint the simple things of life in a straightforward manner, just as he saw them. And it was this very simplicity and charm which were, later, to appeal to so many others.

Early in the year Philip Smith signed a paper to say that Peter's work was up to the standard required by the Association of Mouth and Foot Painting Artists. His painting was then passed by the Association's executive committee as being good enough to compete with that of artists who had no physical handicap.

At the beginning of June in that year, Peter and June were invited to the Association's Conference and Exhibition in Edinburgh. The dinner beforehand was a very congenial affair, with old friends meeting again, new members being drawn into the fold and comparing experiences or spurring each other on with comments on their paintings and achievements. Stegmann, who enjoyed getting the right atmosphere wherever he went, had engaged a piper who piped in the haggis, and everyone cheered spontaneously at this rousing ceremony.

Approaching the Exhibition, Peter glanced up and noticed a large banner which a well-meaning, but misinformed, signwriter had produced. It read, "FOOT and MOUTH Art Exhibition" with the words FOOT and MOUTH prominent in red letters. Peter laughed aloud and turned to June, "I wonder how many farmers will come along to our Exhibition hoping to learn something about cattle disease?"

It is, of course, so simple to reverse the two words, and Peter has often heard people refer to the Association as "The Foot and Mouth Artists". It seems to slip more readily from the tongue. Or perhaps it has just received more publicity!

The Exhibition was opened at the Lyceum Gallery by Earl Haig, himself a painter of repute, and the conference was held at the George Hotel. Erich Stegmann presided over the meeting looking every inch a leader of men, thought Peter. Stegmann said in his report:

"The past three years have proved that, through membership of the Association, a member can live free from worries, be independent, and devote all his time to his job as an artist... Successful exhibitions have been held throughout Europe, reproductions of members' and students' work have been published in fourteen different countries.

"The activities of the Association have been mentioned in the press and on T.V. and film all over Europe. Albert Schweitzer said of our work:

'The pictures give you an idea of the artistic capability of the people who painted them, but something else is shown – courage to live. This is a spiritual gift which we have to accept from the artists and many will be thankful for it.'"

Later, Peter met two other English artists who were present. Richard Hext, born paralysed in Ashburton, Devon, in 1901, was one of the first English artists to join the Association. A benign and lovable man, he gained much pleasure from painting delightful scenes of the gentle Devon countryside where he had lived all his life, looked after by his elderly mother.

The Hext family had lived in extreme poverty, first on a farm labourer's wage and then, when the father was killed, on even less. At the age of seven, after several operations, Hext could stand and walk a little, but nothing could be done for his arms which were without muscles. So he learnt to paint with his mouth. He told Peter with ingenuous pride that two of his pictures had been accepted by the Royal family, and their framed letters of thanks adorned his walls.

"I used to sell paintings for a few shillings to local

tourists," he said, "but since I have been a member of the Mouth and Foot Painters' Association they market all my work and I can now afford to support my old mother and my invalid brother in reasonable comfort. It is a wonderful feeling after all these years."

The other English artist Peter met was Albert Baker. A short stocky man, tough, independent, determined and cheerful, although life had treated him far from gently. He was born with deformed legs and arms and spent most of his stoical childhood in various hospitals and institutions enduring one operation after another – twenty-two in all. He was finally fitted with orthopaedic boots and rigid leg irons, and gradually learned to walk, and then to paint with his mouth. Finally, in 1956, Albert was admitted to Le Court, one of the Cheshire Homes in Hampshire, as an incurable.

"I thought I was finished then," he told Peter, "but actually it was the beginning of a new life. For some time I had been painting water colour cards and selling them at 1s each, but they took me hours to do and I couldn't turn out more than seven a week. Then Erich Stegmann saw some of them and offered me a scholarship so that I could have art training.

"Now, at last," he said with pride, "I am independent. I no longer live on charity, but since joining the Association I can pay my way. Although if it hadn't been for the Cheshire Home I wouldn't be able to do what I'm doing now. If you are one hundred per cent disabled most institutions think all you are fit for is to vegetate. I'm working hard to produce as many paintings as possible, and saving what I can in the hope of eventually being able to buy my own car."

"Good for you," said Peter.

"Good for Stegmann!" corrected Albert. "He's one of the greatest philanthropists I've ever met. What more charitable act can you do than to restore a man's faith and confidence in himself, or give it to him if he has lacked it before? He gave me self-respect, which I've never known before. I felt so useless that I thought of doing away with myself. The greatest charity anyone can give a person is to give them self-respect, and what better way than to enable them to earn their own living."

Peter nodded. "I agree entirely. He's also a brilliant artist. The range of his ability is tremendous, whether it's a large oil painting or a small water colour, a lithograph, a woodcut, or even a sculpture. All of it is first class art. I compare Erich Stegmann with Douglas Bader. Where Bader conquered Flight, Stegmann conquered Art, the physical handicaps really becoming secondary."

It was at the Edinburgh Conference that Peter was made a full member of the Association. This meant that he would in future receive a regular salary, half salary for the first year and full salary thereafter, with the possibility of an annual bonus for additional art work and any extra tasks undertaken on behalf of the Association. He could also vote and have a say in the actions and development of the Association.

It was a very satisfying occasion, an important turning point in Peter's life and one step nearer, he felt, to winning acceptance in the world at large once more.

Chapter Eleven

"IF YOU tune in to the B.B.C. Northern Home Service tonight you will hear all about a remarkable young Wallaseyan who employed guts and imagination to adapt himself to life without arms after a war time crash in the R.A.F.

"The programme, 'Where There's a Will', concerns the 'personal stories of individuals who have triumphed over adversity', and Peter Spencer's victory over his handicap has certainly been triumphant ... From the five minute interview there emerges the portrait of a man who has just never had time to feel sorry for himself." So said the local Wallasey and Liverpool press in August 1959.

This was just one of many interviews and occasional television appearances which Peter was to make, continuing his policy of not retreating from life but of demonstrating to others, including those similarly afflicted, what might be done, given the will and adaptability.

It was at the end of this year that Peter's life took a completely new turn. In November he organised an exhibition of paintings by the Mouth and Foot Painting Artists at the Central Library in Wallasey. The work of eighteen international artists were represented, including those of three Swedish artists: Eva Thor, who not only painted, but had learnt to sew, embroider and write with her mouth; Sune Fick, and Elof Lundberg. Peter had not yet met these artists, but he knew that Sune Fick was born paralysed and had been tied since early childhood to a wheelchair. A handsome young man with a ready wit, Sune was fortunate in being the centre of a loving and united family. When he first started to paint with his mouth, his mother had to hold him in her arms, for his whole body shook convulsively with the strain, but with constant practice he had learnt to paint without support, and now his beautiful paintings of the Swedish forests and streams were commanding high prices.

Elof Lundberg's was a very different story. One of eight, an unwanted child, born paralysed and with a squint, he never received a kind word from his mother, who regarded him with acute distaste. Put in a Home at the age of six, he was taught to draw and write with the mouth. He then endured a series of twenty operations to straighten his feet and legs till he could run and walk.

But his mother would have nothing to do with him. He was kicked and cursed and finally put in a Home for the incurable and insane, where life was of such horror that on three occasions he tried to kill himself. At nineteen, he found himself on the street, totally alone in the world.

But Lundberg possessed a beautiful baritone voice. His landlady befriended him, and he earned a few kronen singing at funerals and weddings. With the brush held in his mouth, he also painted postcards which he sold in the streets. Then Lundberg met Erich Stegmann who saw that he had talent. He was given a scholarship by the Association and, after art training, was made a full member.

When Peter met Lundberg later he found it difficult to believe that his early life had been so harsh. Lundberg had the appearance of a well-tailored, successful business man, he spoke a little English, had a grand sense of fun, and was always ready for a joke and a laugh. Since joining the Association Lundberg had married and produced

This portrait of June's father won Peter a prize in an open exhibition on Merseyside.

Photo by Walter McEvoy

Peter with the painting of BLESMA's coat-of-arms, now hanging in the BLESMA home at Blackpool. While staying there, he proposed to June.

Belfast freighter taking off. Painting by Peter of one of his favourite subjects.

Photo by Walter McEvoy

At a Mouth & Foot Painting Artists Exhibition, Peter shows David Singleton some of the pictures. Encouraged by Peter, he later became an accomplished foot painting artist and a member of the Association.

Photo by Medley & Bird

Robin's toys caught Peter's eye and resulted in this painting.

a family. He had also bought a house outside Stockholm which, in gratitude and affection, he had named Stegmann's Rest.

"It is," he told Peter with a beaming smile, "the most beautiful place in the world!"

Peter himself had eight paintings on exhibition at the library, although only one for sale as all the others were on loan, having been either given away as presents or previously sold. The picture which attracted most attention was a still life of eggs, butter and a loaf of bread, called simply Table Top. Peter enjoyed painting everyday subjects which made a direct, uncomplicated statement. His paintings were skilful and appealing. They came from the heart and were received with affection. They also reproduced extremely well and were to become very popular with the public. His first picture to be reproduced in the Association's calendar was of a single geranium in a flower pot, standing on a sheet of newspaper. It was an emotive painting of great charm.

One of the youngest and most enthusiastic visitors to the Exhibition was David Singleton, who came from Liverpool. A twelve-year-old spastic, unable to use his hands, he had begun to paint instinctively with the brush held in his foot. Having read about David's painting when he won a prize in a children's competition, Peter had invited him to come along.

"Your work shows distinct promise," he told David, "and the Association would like to help you through their Trust Fund."

David progressed so well that he was eventually granted a scholarship, the first step towards becoming a full member of the Association.

The Trust Fund for the Training of Handicapped Children in Arts and Crafts had been formed in 1957, and Peter had later been appointed trustee. The Association do not accept donations as they are not a charity, so any donations which do come in are automatically passed on to the Fund to assist disabled children. Peter was able to distribute this in diverse ways: one contribution went to the Save the Children Fund to assist handicapped children in Morocco. In their letter of appreciation they wrote to Peter:

"We thank you most sincerely for your gift ... we believe very much that music, painting and all other arts and crafts play an important part in the treatment and indeed in the growth of handicapped children, and we are constantly trying to establish this idea at the Rehabilitation Centre in Fez."

He was also able to provide a kiln, pottery equipment and paints for children's homes, including Elmfield School for the Disabled in Harpenden, where the Fund was able to help young Roy Thompson who was born paralysed but began painting with the brush in his mouth from the age of four. Roy enjoyed painting landscapes bold in colour and modern in form, and when he had developed sufficiently was adopted as a student member of the Association.

Peter also gave advice, encouragement and gifts to private individuals. One letter of thanks said simply:

"Your letter suggesting how Edith might use a plastic mouthpiece to write with her mouth has given her a new lease in life. Today she signed a document with the pen held between her teeth, something she would not have attempted a few weeks ago."

At the opening of the Exhibition at the Central Library, the Vice Chairman of the Libraries Committee, under whose jurisdiction the exhibition was being held, introduced Peter by announcing:

"And here is Mr. Peter Scott!"

In those days Peter was not as well known in Wallasey as he is now. He was tempted to ask, "Are you trying to give me the bird?" but tactfully refrained and, instead, made a short speech thanking the Corporation for the use of their room and telling those present a little about the Association of Mouth and Foot Painting Artists.

Bill Baker, one of the Councillors in the audience, was so impressed with his speech and its delivery that shortly afterwards he rang Peter and enquired whether he would be interested in standing for the Council.

"You're just the sort of man we want," he told Peter. "Young blood, and somebody with vision."

Peter was quite shaken by this request. It was something he had never even contemplated. At first he turned down the invitation, but eventually Councillor Baker talked him round by pointing out that he would be doing a service to the community. So Peter agreed to go along to a meeting and make a speech. He was to represent South Liscard which contained Wesley Avenue where he was born. Another prospective candidate was at the meeting complete with several of his friends, and when it came to the vote he got the candidature.

So that, thought Peter, is the end of that.

But he was wrong. The following day someone else from the Conservative Committee phoned him and said they would like him to stand for Marlowe Ward.

Peter's reply was negative, he didn't think he was interested. But that evening the Chairman of Marlowe Ward Conservatives, then Councillor Tomkins, came round to see him, and after an extended chat Peter agreed to stand.

Then came the hard work. For over two months Peter went canvassing from door to door, accompanied by Councillor Tomkins or another helper who introduced him as the new candidate. Together they knocked on over two thousand doors, covering every house in the Ward. Peter was surprised at how many people appeared to know him, there were old school friends and fathers of

131

old school friends, and friends of his parents or of June. When people asked him, "Do you think you're going to get in?" he would reply, smiling, "Well, I don't know. I'm quietly confident."

As his opponent had been on the Council for the past three years, Peter felt that it could have gone either way. Some of the voters' remarks amazed him.

"Ooh, I'm sorry . . . No, I couldn't say. My husband's out at the moment. I would have to talk with him before we decide how we're going to vote."

"Mrs. Pankhurst would turn over in her grave if she heard you say that!" was Peter's reply.

But he did not really mind the canvassing; on the whole he rather enjoyed it. There was no actual speech-making during the campaign. Experience had taught the old hands that if they hired a hall and arranged speeches no one would turn up to listen. The electorate were too busy watching television or football matches to take much interest in local politics.

Peter's opponent was a man named William Peter, and when the day of the election arrived the electors saw on their ballot papers in block capitals, the two words:

PETER
SPENCER

To this day, he wonders how much, or how little, this coincidental similarity of names affected the vote

For Peter Spencer won the election. On the 12th May, 1960, he became Councillor Spencer of Marlowe Ward, with a majority of 249, which was a fair achievement, in view of the fact that only fifty per cent of the electorate managed to get to the polls.

But this was only the beginning.

In October 1959 Peter had presented the British Limbless Ex-Service Men's Association with a large-sized painting of the heraldic Coat of Arms. "A marvellous piece of work both in the colouring and precision of the drawing" reported BLESMAG, the Association's Journal. In January 1960 Peter was made President and Chairman of the Merseyside Branch of BLESMA and, shortly after being elected Councillor in May, he was appointed Vice Chairman of the Libraries Committee.

At the second meeting of this Committee, almost before he had time to learn the ropes, Peter found himself in the chair owing to the illness of the Chairman. Being a "new boy" it was a slightly nerve-wracking experience, but he got on well with the chief librarian and his deputy and the whole proceedings went off quite smoothly.

He also became a member of the Town Planning Committee and, in the end, was serving on a number of different committees on behalf of the council. These new responsibilities combined with his other occupations absorbed most of his evenings as well as his days, but Peter did not resent this as he found that apart from the interest it gave him, the increased activity helped to keep his mind off the pain from the phantom limb which he still experienced, although fortunately not quite as acutely as in the early years after his accident.

While all this was going on, June was looking after the home and Robin, and busily rehearsing the female lead of Magnolia in "Showboat". This production was part of Wallasey's Borough Charter Jubilee Celebration and was being presented by three combined local operatic societies with a cast of over a hundred. She had seven weeks' rehearsals from May to June and the house was a hive of activity, filled with colourful costumes, trilling soprano notes, electioneering pamphlets, and June singing some of the songs from the show to amuse Robin. There was never a dull moment.

"June Lynette's duet 'You are Love' with George Audley provides the high musical moment of the production" said the drama critic in the local paper when the show was produced in June.

That summer Peter and June had an unexpected holiday in Copenhagen while Beatrice Spencer looked after Robin, who was now just over two, a bright, sturdy, alert little boy with his father's direct grey-eyed gaze and the same determined set to his chin that Peter had as a child. On his second birthday for the benefit of his grandparents and great grandmother who was now eighty-five, Peter recorded Robin reciting poetry on the tape recorder with the same clear diction and unruffled self-confidence as his father.

Early that August Peter's pilot friend, Keith Leigh, phoned Peter out of the blue and said there were two seats available on a cheap trip to Copenhagen. Would they like them?

"Wait a moment," said Peter. "I'll ask June. When is it?"

"Tomorrow."

"Tomorrow!" In three minutes Peter was back. "June says, 'Fine!' How long have we got?"

"Exactly twelve hours."

June hurriedly made the arrangements, Peter's parents were delighted to help, and twelve hours later they were sitting in a D.C.4 headed for Copenhagen. The weather was extremely rough, but they landed safely and then had the task of finding somewhere to stay, for there had been no time to book an hotel. They were advised to try Grand Central Station where there was a bureau of accommodation. As June was sitting on a seat feeling far from well after her trip, a stranger approached her, smiling sympathetically.

"Are you looking for accommodation?" June said that they were. "Everywhere is full," said this young woman, "but if you would like to come back to our flat we will be glad to put you up for a couple of days."

So off they went. Always adaptable and quick to make friends, they got on spendidly with this couple and their son Paul, and on the second day they were told:

"We are going away for a few days, but you are welcome to stay in our flat for as long as you like. As we also own the greengrocer shop downstairs, just tell them who you are and help yourself to anything you wish."

Peter and June accepted this generous hospitality gratefully, and spent the next eight days exploring Copenhagen with its fascinating art galleries, museums, shops and nearby beaches, and the unique Tivoli Pleasure Gardens with its hundreds of fairy lights glittering in the dark.

They plied their Danish hosts with gifts on their return and made them promise to come and stay with them when they were in England. Then back they went to Wallasey to fling themselves once more into the maelstrom of life and work which awaited them there.

Chapter Twelve

In April of the following year, Peter gave his first lecture.
It was to the Women's Derby Luncheon Club, and he
had light-heartedly entitled the talk "For Pete's Sake". To
his suppressed amusement, however, when the chairman
introduced him she announced, "And now Mr. Peter
Spencer will give his talk, For the Love of Mike!"

Peter got to his feet. "I don't know anyone by the name
of Mike, but I do know Pete . . . !"

His talk was concerned with all the various associations
with which he had been connected since his accident and
which helped handicapped people, and it was so successful that he began to receive further requests for lectures,
until in the end he was giving eighteen to twenty a year.

The requests came from many quarters: clubs, guilds,
churches, schools, occupational therapists, and Peter
varied his talks accordingly. Some were about his own
experiences, or about BLESMA and similar bodies, and
many concerned the work of the Association of Mouth
and Foot Painting Artists, which he would illustrate with
coloured slides of the artists and their work.

All this he did in a voluntary capacity, although he was
always delighted when some society magnanimously
handed him two or three guineas which he was able to
pass on to BLESMA or to help swell the Trust Fund for
Handicapped Children.

Peter enjoyed giving these talks and meeting the different people involved, but there was one snag. If the organisation was far afield, he had to find someone who was prepared to drive him there, look after him, and if necessary stay the night. Some people, too, expected rather a lot of him.

On one occasion Peter drove a hundred and fifty miles in a hired car to give a talk at a school in the Midlands. He arrived at one o'clock after a tiring journey, to be told that he was expected to give his *first* talk at one-thirty. After a very hasty lunch he did this, and was then requested to give the same talk all over again to a second batch of girls! Most people, fortunately, did not demand quite so much of him.

Meanwhile, June was being kept equally busy.

In May of that year the *Liverpool Echo* carried the following report:

"Into a ward of Leasowe Hospital, Wirral, where all the patients are bed ridden, walked half a dozen cheerful people. Their spokesman told the ward: 'We have come to try to entertain you for a while.' An hour later, when their show ended, the entertainers reaped the reward for their efforts. 'Please,' begged the patients, some with tears of happiness in their eyes, 'please come again soon. It was wonderful!'"

June was one of these travelling troubadors. Since her hospital days she had always had a soft spot for the elderly and infirm, and she found this a most rewarding experience. The show, which was presented at various hospitals by the Red Cross Entertainers of Wallasey, was the idea of Len Makinson who was also the pianist.

Peter and June had known Len Makinson for some time. He was a kindly, warm hearted man and had become a very good friend to both of them. Peter had first met him while serving on the Red Cross Appeals and Entertainment Committee. One of Len's good deeds was to organise the Mile of Pennies annually for the Red Cross. But after an operation on his throat Len found it difficult to use his voice, and asked Peter to do some "barking" for him, enticing the public to throw pennies on to sheets spread across the pavement. So Peter made a tape recording:

> "Please help the Red Cross to help you. We urgently need 58,688 of your pennies to make just one mile!"

When this was broadcast from the top of a van which toured Wallasey and the surrounding district, the pennies came rolling in.

Later, at a Red Cross party, Len found that because of the operation on his throat, he no longer had the power in his voice to control a crowd, and he often remembers the following incident.

"I went to my wife in desperation and told her, 'I'm no damn use to anyone'.

" 'You mustn't lose your temper like that,' a quiet voice said behind me. 'It will get you nowhere. I know.'

"I looked round," says Len, "to see Peter standing behind me, smiling at me, and suddenly I felt very humble.

"Peter has no inhibitions about his disability at all," explained Len. "Some people are embarrassed at first when they meet him. Then they realise they are the only ones to be embarrassed, and they relax.

"Peter is a very sound man with an excellent sense of humour. He knows what he wants in life, and he is a perfectionist in everything he undertakes. He's also a straight talker. If he thinks there is anything wrong with the music, he says so quite bluntly, but he is never rude.

"June, too, is a perfectionist. When she rehearses with me we have to go over and over the song until she feels it is right. And she turns the family out like a new pin. They are a grand couple. I once said to June, 'Peter was very lucky to marry you.' 'No,' she corrected me, 'I was very lucky to marry Peter.'"

In June of that year Peter was chosen to be a delegate to the Vienna Conference of the Association of Mouth and Foot Painting Artists. He and June travelled from London Airport with Hext and Baker. It was at this conference that Peter met Eugene Pirard, a talented and charming Belgian artist, and one of the original members of the Association. His paintings, which displayed great feeling and sensitivity, were landscapes of woodland and heath in every mood and season.

Pirard had been paralysed by polio at the age of eight and had lain in bed for two years unable to move. His foster parents prayed constantly for his recovery, and twice he was taken to Lourdes. After this he began gradually to improve: first the paralysis of his eyes vanished, then his back and finally his legs. Only his arms remained paralysed.

"For seven years," he told Peter, "I went to the Verviers School of Art where I learned to paint with the brush in the mouth, and also to frame my own pictures. Then came a wonderful happening: the Belgium Government bought six of my paintings. Then they began to appear in exhibitions and I was able to rent a little studio. It was after this that I met Erich Stegmann."

Although he was too modest to say so, Peter also learnt that Pirard had been awarded the Silver Medal by the Paris Society of Art, Science and Literature.

While they were at dinner, Peter noticed with interest that Pirard, like many continentals, openly used a toothpick after the meal; the difference being that he managed this, quite unobtrusively, without hands.

Back in their hotel room, June put some toothpaste on to Peter's brush and said, "If Pirard can clean his teeth with a toothpick, why not try a brush?" Peter took the bristles between his teeth and found that by "chewing" and manipulating the brush with his tongue and jaws, he was able to clean his teeth quite effectively To clean the front teeth he put the brush on the edge of the basin and gently but firmly rubbed his teeth on the bristles. Then, holding the brush handle between his teeth, he rinsed the bristles under the tap and replaced the brush in the holder on the wall. Finally he rinsed his mouth, and turned off the tap using his right foot.

From that time onwards he brushed his teeth unaided: one less job for June, one more small step along the path to independence.

At the exhibition in Vienna Peter studied the other members' paintings with interest, noting the different techniques: the delicate flower studies of Riek de Vos, a Dutch mouth painter; the warm Impressionistic paintings dappled with light of Pieter Moleveld, a paralysed foot artist also from Holland; the bold paintings of gauchos and the Argentinian landscape by Enrique Mate; the colourful Austrian scenes of Erich Macho, who was also a crack shot and a graphological wonder despite the fact that he had been born without hands; and the beautiful Norwegian landscapes of Rolf Thomassen, a paralysed teacher of art, who coaxed appealing tunes from the zither with a stick held in his mouth.

While there, Peter and June took a day long trip through the fascinating "Sound of Music" country, and as soon as he returned to Wallasey inspired by all that he had seen, Peter painted a magnificent study of the Austrian Tyrol, with pine covered mountains, snow-capped, a tiny village nestled in the foothills, and the river winding its peaceful way across the plain, which was later reproduced in one of the Association's calendars.

On March 17th, 1962, a baby girl was born to Peter and June, and they named her Jill after "Jill-all-Alone" and Rosemary after Peter's grandmothers. June did not go to bed at all on the night of March 15th. Instead she washed her hair and made some curtains. Early the following morning she told Peter, "I think the baby's on the way".

Peter immediately 'phoned the hospital, and his mother, always a tower of strength in an emergency, came round to hold the fort.

Off June went, not in the least nervous or frightened. She had been doing special exercises ever since she had known the baby was on the way, and was feeling on top of her form. Although it was thirty-six hours before Jill was actually born, June found having a baby a fascinating experience and took a lively interest in the proceedings.

She put on all her make-up just before the birth and Peter was with her up until the last moment. At one stage, June grabbed his toe and hung on to it hard.

"Do they set broken toes here?" joked Peter.

They turned him out just before the actual birth, but he was able to hear Jill's first cry, a very reassuring sound.

"We've got a little girl!" said June when he returned. "Isn't it marvellous?"

Peter was overjoyed. Now they were a real family, a complete unit. Never had he dreamed when he lay powerless in a hospital bed in Halton seventeen years earlier that his future life could hold such fulfilment and happiness.

Robin, too, was delighted to have a baby sister. When June climbed out of the car on her return home from hospital, she handed the baby to Joyce Ellison, the friend who had come with her, and went forward to greet her small son. But Robin rushed past her, crying excitedly, "Where's Jill? Where's Jill!"

Now June really had her hands full. But she was never one to shirk hard work. Efficient and energetic, she looked after Peter and the children, washed, cleaned, cooked huge appetising meals, baked her own bread and cakes and sank into bed exhausted at the end of the day.

Peter, too, worked like a Trojan; painting, giving talks and elocution lessons, attending innumerable committee meetings, sometimes as many as six or eight in a week, and acting as Liaison Officer for the London Office of the Association of Mouth and Foot Painting Artists, answering many of the letters which came to the office with queries about the artists and their work.

In May, Peter was made Governor of Oldershaw Grammar School and of the Wallasey School of Art, where he found himself in the interesting position of being a student and Governor at the same time.

Then, concerned that Wallasey did nothing to encourage the arts, Peter suggested to the Library Committee that an exhibition of paintings by local artists might be held in the Central Library. The first exhibition was opened by the Mayor, Alderman C. G. E. Dingle, on April 28th. This created so much interest locally that a Wallasey Art Society was formed, of which Peter was asked to be Chairman, and the following summer they held their first Open Air Exhibition in New Brighton on the Left Bank of the Mersey. The exhibition was so successful that it became an annual event, and a very pleasant occasion too, with the band playing in the background, the water lapping the embankment, and a colourful array of paintings hanging on the railings.

Some of the public comments were more concerned with the subject than with the painting.

"Gor!" Peter heard one lad say. "Look; she's got no clothes on."

Or, when one of the viewers spied a particularly abstruse abstract, "Coo! What d'you think that's supposed to be? Looks like one of little Freddie's scribbles".

Little did they know that the artist was probably standing right behind them. On the whole, though, the comments were tolerably well informed, and a fair number of the paintings were sold.

During the summer Peter received a letter from an American clergyman, the Reverend Harold Wilke, who had read about Peter in an Indian magazine for the disabled when he was in Bombay.

"We have something in common," he wrote. "I'm shortly coming to England and would very much like to meet you."

So in August of that year Len Makinson drove Peter to meet his American visitor at Liverpool Airport, where they saw a well-built, good-looking man in his forties coming towards them.

"Harold Wilke?" asked Peter.

"Well, hello there, Peter! I recognise you from your photo. Nice to meet you at last. But, gee! you shouldn't have bothered to meet me. I would have gone over the Mersey on the ferry and taken the bus to your house," said Wilke with a genial smile.

As soon as they were in the car, Wilke opened his knapsack with his toes and filled and lit his pipe in the same manner. The fact that he was born without arms appeared in no way to hamper his mobility. He kept his loose change in his shoe, flicked his wallet out of his jacket with his foot, and deftly signed traveller's cheques with a pen held in his toes.

Wilke was an expert in rehabilitation and had written a thought-provoking book about it. He had also travelled the world, been in the U.S. Army, and had produced five sons.

"I left my wife with friends in London," he told Peter, "while I took a plane to Scotland and visited some disabled people I know there."

Because he had been without arms since birth, Wilke had learnt from the beginning, while his body was still young and supple, to use his feet for his requirements. It is not so easy to adapt one's body or retrain the muscles once one has left childhood behind.

A man of great charm, Wilke was a humanitarian and a philosopher, having come completely to terms with his disability at a very early age. He also had a great sense of humour, and Peter and June were sorry to see him go.

"Be sure to come and see us if ever you're in the States again," said Wilke on parting.

"We certainly will if we ever get the opportunity," promised Peter, little knowing that within three years he and June would be in New York, walking down Fifth Avenue with Harold Wilke beside them.

It was a suggestion from Harold Wilke which on one occasion brought Peter under the suspicion of the authorities. With his brother-in-law Ken, he arrived in the early hours of the morning at Manchester Airport after a tiring night flight from Spain. They presented their cases for inspection at the Customs desk and, much to their surprise and annoyance, had to pay 38s duty on a bottle which they thought, in all innocence, would be duty free. Having finally been cleared and the bags given the magic chalk marks, Ken moved off with two cases, leaving Peter with one other. He was pushing the case along the floor with his foot when suddenly the same Customs officer appeared by his side.

"Can I carry your bag for you, sir?"

"That's very kind of you," said Peter, thinking he wasn't such a bad chap after all.

He followed the officer and his case, expecting to go down the stairs to where Ken would now be with the car. But to his amazement he found himself in a small room with a second Customs officer and the door closed behind him. They looked him straight in the eye.

"Have you declared everything, sir?"

"Yes."

"Everything on your person, sir?"

"Yes."

"Would you mind if we searched you, sir?"

Peter was beginning to find this questioning and the repetitive "sir" as surprising and annoying as the duty they had been charged, but with commendable self-control refrained from comment.

"No, I've no objection."

"Would you mind putting your left foot up on that stool, sir?"

Peter did so. Then with a sudden flash of illumination he realised what it was all about. His watch! Emulating Harold Wilke, he was wearing it on the left ankle.

"Oh, that . . . !" he said, and explained.

"I see, sir." The officer examined the watch closely, as if doubting Peter's word. "One of our men spotted it on your ankle."

"Full marks to your man," said Peter coldly. He was tempted to add facetiously, "It's the watches strapped round my thigh that I find most uncomfortable," but thought better of it. They might have wanted to take his trousers off!

"May I go now?" he asked.

"Certainly." The unsmiling officer, seemingly disappointed at the result of the interview, opened the door and Peter finally rejoined Ken.

"Whatever happened to you?"

"They nearly grabbed me as an international smuggler," said Peter with a smile. "I wonder if Harold Wilke ever has this trouble. . . ?"

Chapter Thirteen

In May of that year Peter was re-elected councillor for Marlowe Ward, doubling his majority, and in June he attended the Mouth and Foot Painting Artists' Exhibition and Conference in Madrid with Ken, as June was unable to leave Jill.

The journey to Madrid was full of incident. The Vanguard was late taking off from Manchester to Paris, and Peter and Ken missed their connection as no one had informed them that it was necessary to change airports at Paris. The only available plane did not leave till late that night, and when they arrived there was only one first class seat instead of the two tourist they had booked.

"Well, you go on that," said Ken, "and we'll just have to hope that someone will be able to look after you the other end."

However, a few minutes before the plane took off, a tourist passenger cancelled his seat and Ken was able to have it. Peter's luggage was missing when they landed at the airport and not re-discovered until some time after they reached the terminal. As a consequence they did not reach their hotel in Madrid until ten p.m. and so missed the Association's dinner, which was very disappointing as Erich Stegmann always made this quite an occasion, and Peter enjoyed meeting and having a congenial chat with the other members with whom he shared so much.

However, the rest of the visit went off very well. Peter

was able to attend both the conference and exhibition, and to converse with several of the members whom he had not previously met. Notably Athol Thompson, a brawny, cheerful, extrovert artist from Australia, who had lost his arms at the age of eight after touching a high tension cable.

"It's the first time I've been able to come to a conference," Athol told Peter, "because the distance I have to travel makes it rather expensive. But I'm really thrilled at being able to talk to and exchange ideas with so many of the other artists."

"When we're all gathered together like this it resembles a little United Nations," said Peter. Athol laughingly agreed.

Peter found they had many things in common. Athol was not only a councillor and a mouth painter but he was also married to a girl called June. However, he had four children to Peter's two, and his wife did several things for him which Peter had learnt to manage by himself, such as feeding him, whereas Peter now got down to his food unaided.

"I've had a pretty varied career," Athol told Peter. "First I was engaged in commercial design, then during the war I was a professional singer touring the army camps. After that I became a civil servant. And now I paint, garden, swim and," he laughed heartily, "train parakeets to talk."

Peter knew that Athol was also an expert mouth-writer and a successful artist who enjoyed nothing more than painting vast landscapes of the Australian bush.

Another interesting artist Peter met in Madrid was Manuel Parreno, son of a Spanish shoemaker, born with paralysed arms. As he had only recently been married, Peter had brought him a typically English gift of wedgwood china, with which he was delighted.

147

"What do they think of your paintings in Spain?" Peter asked.

"I have won top prizes for some of my work," said Manuel, "but some people are envious. They say I only sell my paintings because of the way they are painted ... with the foot."

Peter shrugged. "You will always find that. Take no notice. Those with intelligence and understanding know better. Your work has great depth and feeling and I am not surprised that it is highly spoken of."

While Peter was at the Exhibition looking at the paintings, a voice behind him said, "Good, aren't they!" and he turned round to see the English artist, Albert Baker, whom he had first met in Edinburgh.

"Nice to see you!" said Peter. "How's it going? Have you been able to buy that car yet?"

"Yes!" said Baker with the smile of a conqueror. "What a difference it makes. It's marvellous to be able to drive around the countryside instead of being confined to one room all day. I've had it specially adapted because of my leg irons. I can't bend them at the knee and it's murder sitting on an ordinary seat. I'm hoping to get a little electric car eventually, that I can drive myself, adapted to my own specification. The Ministry of Health are being very sticky about it. They don't seem to think I can manage it. But I'm not giving up."

Peter shook his head. "Never give up. Have you learnt to type yet?"

"I don't have much need of it. I write with the pen in my mouth in block capitals, as I've always done. My ordinary writing is like a doctor's ... you can't read it! But I can shave myself with an electric razor and comb my hair. I've got a comb on the end of a rod attached to the bed rail. I've just got back from the football match. Real Madrid. Did you go?"

"No," said Peter. "Ken and I wanted to look round the town."

"It was pretty rough. I nearly got crushed by the crowd when they started to fight all around us. I would have done if my friend hadn't leant his body across me to protect me. It was an ugly moment." Albert laughed heartily. "But I'm all in one piece. Oh! There's Athol. Must have a word with him," and Baker stumped off, cheerful and indomitable.

Glancing down the room, Peter caught sight of an old friend, Cefischer. He hurried towards him.

"Hello, there!" In friendly greeting Peter touched Cefischer's shoulder with his own.

"We meet again!" Cefischer, a big masculine man with horn-rimmed glasses and a thrusting determined jaw, acknowledged him with a smile.

"I've been admiring your painting, 'The Dream,' said Peter. "It is really original, with the boy dreaming over his book and all the characters springing to life, just as he imagines them . . ."

"You like it? I am glad."

Before the second world war Cefischer had been art editor on a well-known German magazine, but during an air raid his arms had been torn off by a bomb splinter. The thought flashed through Peter's mind that, had he been a bomber pilot, one of his bombs could have been responsible for the injury inflicted on this man who was now his friend. It brought home to him even more intensely the total futility of war.

At first, after his terrible injuries, Cefischer had thought his life was over. Then, when eventually he began to readjust to the situation, he remembered a painter he had once met on holiday in Mittenwald: Erich Stegmann who painted with his mouth and ignored his disability.

"Why not?" thought Cefischer.

Spurred on by his wife, he gradually taught himself to

paint in this new way, until at last his work had reached the same high standard as before his accident. His former editor was delighted to have him back and he created a new humorous character: Oscar the Tom Cat. Then he met Erich Stegmann and joined the Association. The cards Cefischer painted for the Association were very popular and he particularly enjoyed depicting young animals in action or in humorous situations.

Peter and his brother-in-law returned home from the Madrid Conference the following day, and throughout 1964 he and June continued to work like beavers, from the time they got up in the morning till they went to bed at night.

Despite all this activity, Peter always managed to find time for the children. Robin was now a high-spirited six-year-old, while Jill was two, a little blonde bombshell with laughing blue eyes. With her reins fastened around his wrist, Peter would take Jill to the park where she clambered on to a seat, while Peter bent down so that she could be carried around gleefully on his shoulders. Later he would have a swift game of football with Robin, and on the way home they would call and see the grandparents. Peter usually managed to drop in for a coffee or a brief chat with his parents on most days, for they only lived five minutes away. Often on Sunday mornings he and Robin would go to the swimming-pool and have races or join in the activities of the Disabled Persons Swimming Club.

In the following year, Peter was asked by the Association to attend an Exhibition at The Art Gallery in Cheddar, Somerset, where eighty paintings were on view. As a public relations man, the Association now considered Peter to be first-class. He was efficient, industrious and completely natural.

One of the paintings on view was by Junkyo Ohishi of Japan, and Peter thought her story a particularly inspiring one. Born in 1888, at the age of seven Junkyo's arms were cut off by her step-father who went mad and attacked his entire family with a Japanese sword. Junkyo survived and as a young girl she earned a living dancing and singing with a travelling theatre.

Today, Peter was aware that she was not only a talented mouth-artist and gracious hostess to the famous, but as a Buddhist priestess she devoted much of her time to copying out sacred writings, teaching handicapped children to write and paint, and caring for the sick and disabled to whom most of her money was given.

Jim Driver was another interesting exhibitor. Peter felt quite close to this artist, for although they had not met, they had recently started corresponding by sending tape-recorded messages to each other, a method of communication which Peter considered had more warmth – and was also simpler – than typewritten letters, although both were skilled typists.

Jim Driver had told Peter all about his life in New Zealand where he had been paralysed by polio as a boy. Movement and feeling gradually returned to his neck and feet, but his arms remained immobile. Fortunately he had a great sense of humour and found many ways of overcoming his disability.

"Well, Peter, did I tell you about my 'other arms'?" Jim would ask in his good-natured New Zealand accent. "One thing about them, they certainly won't break . . . They're made of steel!" His delighted laughter came booming across the tape.

"Now, these arms of mine, they're upright steel rods, worked by foot, and they have a horizontal rod at the top with which I can tap the typewriter keys, or use to hold a knife and fork, or to frame my pictures.

"I won't say I don't miss my arms. Which of us doesn't, Peter? It's something we never quite get used to. But, like you, I've learnt to make the best of what I've got, to have a good life without them.

"I'm sitting here at the bay window looking out across the sea and the Pacific Islands. I'm very fond of the sea. I hardly ever paint anything else. I spend a lot of time *on* it, too.

"Thought you might like to see the enclosed cutting from the local paper: 'Boatman's spirit conquered sea of troubles'. Quite a good pun. I've got the only foot controlled motorboat in the world. Had it specially adapted. Done a lot of sailing, too. My job's to sit on the windward side with my foot tucked under the stacking-out strap to hold the boat down.

"I've been president of the Otago Idlealong Club several times and am publicity officer and commodore of the Otago Power Boat Club. So, as you can see, I don't have many idle moments. I've also appeared on TV and radio and I write short stories and sports reports. But painting is of course my main occupation, and I can do it either with my mouth or my artificial hands."

In the following years Jim's life became even more full, as he married in 1966, and in 1968 he sent a delighted tape to Peter telling him that he and Dorothy had a baby son.*

During the Cheddar Exhibition Peter was asked to appear on B.B.C. Television at Bristol with the picture he had painted of Churchill in which he tried to include all the things for which Churchill had been famous, and which was later to be hung in Wallasey's Conservative headquarters. No sooner had Peter returned home after this television interview than the commercial television company, T.W.W., 'phoned to say they had heard about the exhibition and would he go down to their studios. So, indefatigable in the cause as ever, off he went once more,

---

* It has since been learned with regret that Jim Driver died suddenly in March 1970.

152

this time accompanied by his old friend Les Laycock.

Peter borrowed some paintings from the exhibition; a still life of bottles and an aircraft painting, and the television interview went something like this:

"Why do you paint aircraft?"

"Because I like them."

"Why do you paint bottles?"

"Because I like the contents!"

They did the journey there and back in a day, eventually reaching home at one o'clock the following morning.

It was in this year that Peter and Len Makinson wrote their first song, "This is my Love". Len wrote the music, Peter put the words to it, and it was sung by June. Later on they wrote a lullaby together called "See you in the Morning", the last words they said to the children before they went to sleep, and Len composed for BLESMA a stirring and moving march "Service and Fortitude", whose chords seemed to speak of goodness, and loving and honouring one's fellow men. At first, however, it was too fast.

"Remember," said Peter, "that you are writing for the disabled. Perhaps something like this," and he struck a chord with his toes.

So Len composed a slow, steady march more suited to the gait of those who had been incapacitated in the war.

It was no longer painful for Peter to listen to others play the piano. He had deliberately eradicated any bitterness he had felt at his loss, and could now listen to Len playing with enjoyment instead of anguish. The two families met often, and there was a spirit of comradeship, good neighbourliness and warmth between them which Peter and June shared with many others in Wallasey.

That summer Peter had his first accident since the tragic one of 1945. He slipped while going from the kitchen into the hall and, without arms to protect himself, crashed his head against the wall and knocked himself unconscious. The shock made him violently sick, his nose bled, his eye went black and closed up, and the right side of his face was temporarily paralysed. He went to bed suffering from shock but within a few hours was up and active again, though he could feel pain in the nerves of his face for many months afterwards.

Peter was too busy planning his visit to Canada and America by then, however, to have time to think of his bruises. He had been selected as delegate to the Association's Conference and Exhibition to be held in Toronto in the autumn, and was hoping to be able to make a brief, nostalgic trip to the scene of his cadet days in the R.A.F. at Clewiston, Florida.

He felt that these Conferences were a very valuable means of putting the members in touch with each other, so that they might see and assess the type of work that was being done. They could criticise, appreciate and discuss each other's paintings, and feel, reassuringly, that they were not isolated but an integral part of a vast but close-knit organisation.

When the Association was in its infancy it was possible, and necessary according to the Statutes to hold a Conference and Annual General Meeting each year, to which all the members were invited. But as the Association grew, and more and more members joined from countries scattered across the globe, this became impossible, and it was agreed for reasons of economy to limit the Conferences to one every three or four years, to which a representative selection of delegates would be invited. International Exhibitions of members' work continued to be held frequently, however, in various parts of the world throughout each year.

For some of the members who were ill or wholly incapacitated it was impossible to travel any distance, but those who could do so came, whatever the planning and difficulties involved, even though it meant travelling in a wheelchair. To all, it was worth the struggle and effort even if they came but once in their lives. Peter knew it was an occasion they never forgot. They were comrades both in art and in spirit. And they always returned home filled with enthusiasm and inspired to do even greater work.

For Peter, as for all members, the act of painting was exhausting and required supreme tenacity and dogged determination. Many could only paint for short spells at a time before they reached exhaustion point and it became necessary to rest before they started once again. Every painting was the outcome of enormous physical and mental strain, the brush guided by the determination not to give in, never to be beaten. For Peter and his fellow artists life could never be easy, but it could be rewarding. And the knowledge of what it had cost in effort made the result even more worthwhile.

As soon as Mr. and Mrs. Nesmith and Peter's other friends in America heard that he was crossing the Atlantic, they insisted with their usual friendly and spontaneous hospitality that he and his wife must go and stay with them. Peter and June left Liverpool on the *Sylvania* in September and a week later, as they stood together on the deck, June caught her first glimpse of the Statue of Liberty and the exciting Manhattan skyline.

Their old friend the Rev. Harold Wilke met them off the boat and immediately whipped them round New York on an instant sightseeing tour. It was quite an experience. New York was like a hot damp oven, and June was wearing a warm autumn suit which felt warmer every minute as they walked along 42nd Street, around Times Square, then up Fifth Avenue to the Rockefeller Centre.

They stopped for lunch; Wilke then returned to his office and Peter and June went on to the beautifully constructed and very exciting United Nations building. The air conditioning was particularly welcome in the heat and humidity, but by then June's feet were "killing her", so she took off her shoes and went round contentedly in her stockinged feet.

There was a water shortage in New York and they were amused to see on the back of one dirty coach the words, "We're not washing so you can!"

Peter was anxious to miss nothing, for they might never be able to come again. They visited museums, theatres, and art galleries non-stop till early evening, when they met Wilke at Grand Central Station. He was one of the several friends who had graciously offered them hospitality, and they travelled by train to his home in White Plains, standing for the thirty minute journey in the intense heat of a train packed to the doors. They slept well that night!

The days flashed by. They met the Mayor, they visited the Metropolitan Museum of Art, they soared to the top of the Empire State building just as the lights were coming on all over the city – a magnificent sight – and then went to see "Hello Dolly" at the St. James'. They had been lucky to get the tickets. All the theatre agents had told them flatly, "No hope."

"Let's try just one more," said Peter, unperturbed, "and I'll speak to them."

He went smiling up to the assistant, and putting on his most English accent said quietly, "Excuse me, but do you happen to have any tickets for the show?"

"Why, yes sir," said the girl, smiling back at him. "We certainly have."

"Well!" Wilke looked at him with amused respect. "I've never seen that happen before."

In the interval Peter turned to Wilke, "Mrs. Nesmith asked me to 'phone her at eight-thirty. It's just about that now."

"Right!" said Wilke. "I'll come with you."

Peter opened the door of the 'phone box with his foot

and together the two armless men crowded into the booth, watched in some amazement by several theatregoers who stood nearby.

"I've got some change," said Wilke, nipping it out of his shoe with his socked foot and pushing it into the slot. "Here you are!" And he whipped the receiver off the hook with his toes and held it up to Peter's ear.

"You must be made of elastic!" said Peter.

He got through to Mrs. Nesmith, arranged what time they would be arriving at the airport in Florida, pushed open the door for Wilke, and together they returned to see the rest of the show.

The following day they visited the World's Fair, including the impressive Churchill Pavilion, which contained seventy of Churchill's original oil paintings, his life story in photographs, and his voice coming through on loud speakers. As soon as darkness fell they climbed to the top of the Observation Tower and saw the whole panorama of New York: the river, the bridges, the buildings all glittering with light, and helicopters and aeroplanes flying overhead. It was all very exciting and they were reluctant to leave.

On their final day they had arranged to meet Stephen Sles, one of the newer members of the Association, at Grand Central Station at four p.m. They had been waiting for some time, when finally a man wearing a coat with two empty sleeves approached them.

"Hello, Mr. Sles!" said Peter. "Nice to meet you."

The man stared at them with hostility. "Whaddaya mean? My name ain't Sles. You got the wrong guy."

He walked away, and as Peter watched him go he realised that both the "guy's" hands were clasped behind his back like the Duke of Edinburgh. With his coat slung over his shoulders this had given him the appearance of being without arms.

Shortly afterwards, Stephen Sles arrived with a friend.

"O.k." said the friend. "I'll drop you here and meet you at 11 o'clock tonight," and he vanished.

Sles was twenty-five and a spastic. He was severely disabled and walked with considerable difficulty, but his mind was brilliant. Born in New Jersey, he had made a study of Plato and other philosophers, as well as of psychology. He spoke fluent French and Spanish, but with a slight slur due to his disability. They spent the afternoon at Radio City, and over dinner Stephen Sles told them something about himself.

"I went to college in the States and then won a scholarship to Madrid University where I studied art. I'd been drawing with the pencil in my mouth since I was six. I'm what's known as an *avant garde* painter, and I like doing," he swung out an arm to demonstrate, "LARGE paintings. I've had paintings on show in a number of exhibitions in the States, Mexico, Spain and so on, where they've been favourably reviewed by the press and television.

"Literature, music, history, politics, I can take an active interest in them all. Had some poetry published, too. So you see I keep pretty busy."

"It's the best way," said Peter. "Then you don't have time to think about your troubles."

"You're exactly right, Peter."

Despite the fact that Sles had not much control over his limbs, he coped quite well with his meal and was able to feed himself to a certain extent.

"What are you doing at the moment?" asked Peter.

"Well, I've been studying art in Paris, and next I'm off to Greece and Spain."

"Quite a globe trotter," commented June.

"It's my policy to keep on the move," Sles said, struggling determinedly to his feet.

Peter and June left White Plains the following day. They were sorry to leave this very friendly family and made Wilke promise to come and see them next time he was in England. Then they stepped on to a Greyhound coach to Philadelphia where they met Thea and Gerry Rogers, an old school friend. Their next port of call was Cleveland where they were to stay with Joe and Barbara Bailey.

Barbara Bailey had written to the Association early in the year asking if she could have the original of one of Peter's Christmas cards, Sunset Glow, a very attractive study of winter trees casting their shadows across the snow. As the original had been damaged, Peter painted a similar scene especially for her. This started up a correspondence between them, which eventually ended by Barbara asking Peter and June to come and stay with them. He took another painting with him to give to Barbara, of Clare Bridge, Cambridge, a delightfully peaceful sunlit scene, which Joe Bailey liked so much that he commissioned a painting of an aircraft. This was a pleasure for Peter, as he always enjoyed painting planes – it was the next best thing to flying one. He liked, and was very successful at creating the sensation of speed and winged movement.

The Baileys were a charming couple with a fine house at Shaker Heights. Peter and June spent a pleasant couple of days with them and then packed their bags and were on their way once more.

"You've been marvellous guests," said Barbara when seeing them off, "and we've been such good friends that I hate to see you go, but I'll look at my pictures and enjoy them for ever."

At nearby Chagrin Falls they were the guests of Gini and Joe Laurie. Gini Laurie was the Managing Editor of the *Toomey J Gazette,* a non-profit making journal produced by a staff of disabled and their non-disabled friends. Its aim was to reach, to inform, and to dignify all severely disabled people throughout the world.

The Lauries had a beautiful home, nine cats who had

a free run of the house, and a swimming pool which was kept permanently at a temperature of 84 degrees. Many of the friends Gini brought home with her were disabled, and swimming was one of their greatest pleasures. Gini was kindness itself. One of her favourite expressions was, "Oh, you are a darrlin!"

While there, Peter gave a talk about his trip and the Association of Mouth and Foot Painting Artists, and then they were off again – this time to Florida. Mr. and Mrs. Nesmith were there to meet them at West Palm Beach Airport. It was a great reunion.

"Wonderful to see you again!" said Mrs. Nesmith hugging them both. She was nearly eighty, but seemed to Peter almost unchanged, and just as friendly and kind as ever.

In the evening Peter gave a talk about the Association to an audience of fifty. He also showed slides of the artists' work, and June sang several songs.

Mrs. Owen, a friend from Clewiston days, drove them the seventy miles to see the No. 5 British Flying Training School where Peter had been a cadet twenty-two years before.

"I must warn you," she said, "that you will see quite a change."

But Peter was not prepared for the sight which met his eyes. It was derelict: overgrown with weeds, windows smashed, broken glass everywhere. The beautiful swimming pool was full of black water – and fish. Only one hangar was still open. The control tower had been blown down in a hurricane, and what was left of it was being used by a small aeroplane company who specialised in parachute training and sky-diving. It was a very sad sentimental journey.

Sometime later Peter was happy to learn from friends in Florida that the airfield had been taken over by the Florida Aeronautical Institute for the specific purpose of

One of Peter's most recent paintings, Tropical Moonlight.

Peter's interest in meteorology is reflected in his painting of Winter Clouds.

training airline pilots, and was to be completely redeveloped and rebuilt.

Peter and June spent several idyllic days with the Nesmiths in Palm Beach, during which time Peter gave several more illustrated talks about the Association. He and June were also requested to broadcast on the local radio station, and an informal reception was held for them at the Palm Beach County Crippled Children's Society.

On October 3rd they flew to Toronto for the forthcoming Conference. Soon after they had settled into their hotel, Peter was called upon to take part in a television interview with Myron Angus, one of the Canadian artists. After introducing them both and explaining that Myron ran an art gallery in Toronto and had been born without the use of either arms or legs, the interviewer turned to Myron.

"Tell me something about the Association, Mr. Angus. Is your work judged by the art critics of the world quite impartially? Or how much is their judgment influenced by the technique you use . . . the fact that you're disabled and unable to paint in the normal way?"

"We hope for a completely impartial judgment, and in most cases feel we get it," said Angus equably. "The majority of our artists have had their work accepted in exhibitions where they've been in open competition with what you call 'normal' artists, and their work therefore judged by people who have been totally unaware that the paintings have been executed without the use of hands. Many of our members have won high awards in the field of art."

"Is that so? But of course in this present exhibition it's made clear that these paintings were not done by the normally accepted method." Then, turning to Peter, he went on, "How many people do you think would look upon this as a stunt, Mr. Spencer?"

"No doubt a certain amount would. It's inevitable. But in the main we're accepted for our worth as artists unrelated to our slightly unusual method of creation," said Peter, who had been asked this same question on so many previous occasions.

At four o'clock that afternoon the Exhibition of Mouth and Foot Painting Artists was officially opened at the Casa Loma, a large house on the outskirts of Toronto, by the Commissioner for Cultural Affairs. This was followed by a speech from the Mayor who spoke in appreciation of the quality of the paintings. As was his custom, Erich Stegmann then drew, with the brush held in his mouth, a lightning portrait of the Mayor and presented it to him as a memento of the exhibition.

Stegmann had been watched with close attention by the press and distinguished guests, and later a photograph of the event appeared in the newspaper, with a bold headline: "LOOK, MA! NO HANDS!" Stegmann was as amused by this black humour as anyone.

Peter enjoyed wandering around the Exhibition and meeting friends old and new, in particular Earl Bailly, one of the most widely known of the mouth painters whose cards Peter had first seen many years ago, little dreaming that one day the two of them would meet as fellow artists.

Earl Bailly, a talented artist who delighted in creating colourful and exuberant scenes of the Novia Scotia land and seascapes, had been paralysed from the age of two, and had painted unceasingly since he was fourteen. His paintings had been bought by the National Gallery in Ottawa as well as by the government and numerous celebrities.

He got on very well with June. Their cheerful spirits and zest for life matched one another and they had plenty of laughs and jokes together. Bailley was touring the Exhibition in his wheelchair when he came across Peter studying one of his paintings.

"I particularly like your use of colour," said Peter.

"Yes, colour fascinates me," admitted Bailly, "but I find oils increasingly difficult to use with the years. The brush feels so heavy in the mouth when loaded with paint. I shall have to resort more and more to water colour. I see you have five paintings in the Exhibition, Peter. This one, Air Canada, is very apt. You certainly have a way with planes."

"They still excite me," admitted Peter. "I'll always love flying, even though I can't take an active part any more."

"Hello, there!" said a genial American voice, and Peter turned round to see Jimmy Rodolfos who had come up behind him in his wheelchair.

"Nice to see you," said Peter, offering his left elbow and touching Jimmy on his left shoulder. Denied the ability to shake hands, it was always doubly important to Peter to make some such contact in order to express his joy at meeting a friend.

Jimmy Rodolfos, one of the American artists, was a big brawny man with thick black hair and brows. His bearded face was alive with good humour and his dark eyes shining with warmth and friendliness, as he introduced Peter to his mother and wife. He and Fay had met while convalescing in the same hospital, Fay from polio and Jimmy from the swimming accident which had paralysed his limbs. Fay, too, was in a wheelchair, but she had the use of her arms.

"Fay drove us part of the way here from Massachusetts in the station wagon," said Jimmy with some pride. "I don't know where some of us would be without our women folk behind us."

"How right you are," agreed Peter.

"We're terribly impressed with the way they've organised this convention," Jimmy went on. "We've never been to anything like it before. And I've had the added pleasure of hearing that one of my paintings has been bought here today."

"Congratulations!" said Peter warmly. " I've just been looking at your painting, Fall Landscape. Did you do it from life?"

"Not quite, Peter. It's difficult for me to do much painting out of doors. Fay and I travel through the mountains and countryside taking colour photos during Summer and Fall when New England is a blaze of colour, and this helps me later to remember the details of the scene.

"It's been wonderful being able to meet all the other artists here, learning about their special problems, and exchanging ideas. I already feel as if I've known Erich Stegmann all my life. He made us feel so much at home, always with a smile on his face and that twinkle in his blue eyes."

That evening at the Association's official dinner in the hotel ballroom Peter was able to chat with Glen Fowler, an American member whom he had met earlier in the day. This artist had fractured his neck in a car accident at the age of sixteen and it had resulted in paralysis of his limbs. A proud, impatient youth, it had turned him into an embittered rebel. Then in 1958 he had married his nurse, Joanne, and life had taken on a happier aspect.

Dark haired and with a thrusting, forceful set to his jaw, Fowler was a touchy man not overburdened with tact, but he was also a gifted artist and a talented interpreter of the American landscape.

"I hear you've recently had a son," said Peter.

Fowler's intense face relaxed into a smile. "Yeah. He's just two months old. We miss him already. But I'm glad I came, I've got a lot of noo ideas now, Peter. It's been a very stimulating occasion, and just as soon as I get back home I'm going to start on some of them."

The Association's Convention was held at nine-thirty the following morning. It was a formal occasion with all

164

the delegates seated around the conference table and Erich Stegmann presiding at the head. The Minutes of the last meeting were read, followed by the President's address, which was given in his native German. This had already been typed and translated into various languages for the benefit of the delegates and was followed by the Treasurer's report. Most of the members made notes during the meeting, some with the pen in their mouth while others, such as Charles Pasche, scribbled furiously away with their feet on the table and the pen held between their toes.

The Convention over, Peter and June made a quick trip to Niagara Falls with some of the other artists. Then they sailed back to England on the *Empress of Canada*, arriving home on October 15th. It was good to see the children again. Robin and Jill were very excited at their return and flung themselves at their parents in an ecstacy of delight. Peter kissed them both and the warmth of his greeting was in his eyes and his smile. June caught them into her arms and hugged them. Bountiful, and boisterous as they, she gave them both big smacking kisses before standing back to survey them.

"You've grown, Robin. I'm sure you have."

"Yes!" said Robin excitedly. "Does it show?"

Peter turned to his parents. "Have they been good?"

"Oh, remarkably so!" said Mr. Spencer with a twinkle in his eyes. "Bursting with life as usual, but it's a pleasure to have them."

"We're really grateful to you both," said Peter. "You know that. It would have been impossible for us to do so many of the things we've done together without your help."

Chapter Fourteen

THE FOLLOWING day Peter and June plunged back into work. Peter's desk was piled high with correspondence which had accumulated in his absence and which he now tackled with fervour. June attacked the household chores and overgrown garden, and threw herself happily into rehearsals for her part as Grace Pritchard in "Love from Judy", which was produced by the Wallasey Operatic Society, at the Royal Court Theatre in Liverpool, at the end of November.

Meanwhile, Peter was busy helping to prepare for Wallasey's first Festival of the Arts. This idea was first mooted in January 1965, when Councillor F. H. Hutty was made Chairman of the committee, E. A. Mongor the Organising Secretary and Peter the Vice-Chairman. By the following October they had organised a wide programme of events which had an overall attendance of nearly eight thousand. The schools production of Benjamin Britten's "Noye's Fludde" was sold out, as were the lectures on Old Wallasey. There was a memorable recital by the Argentinian pianist Martha Argerich, a concert by the Liverpool Philharmonic, a programme of films made by the Wallasey Cine Group, several art exhibitions, and an evening of folk music which proved very popular.

Letters were received from the public expressing their enjoyment, and before it was over in December the members of the committee were already planning their next Arts Festival.

Earlier in the year, during the controversial visit of the Queen and the Duke of Edinburgh to Germany, Peter suggested to BLESMA that it would be an appropriate moment to send a letter of goodwill to their opposite numbers in that country: the German Association of Ex Service and Civilian Victims, with whom they had something in common, all being victims of the war. In reply to his letter Peter received the following from the president of the German organisation:

"You have given us great pleasure with your letter. We thank you very much and would like to say that Her Majesty the Queen has been received with a great wave of sympathy and admiration during her visit to the Federal Republic of Germany. Her Majesty and her husband have conquered the hearts of my countrymen. We are convinced that this visit has done a lot to improve the relationship of our two countries which was darkened through two wars.

We return your greetings and goodwill message and share your opinion that people who became victims of the wars should maintain friendly contacts with each other."

Herr Kleine's letter ended, "In friendship".

Peter felt certain that such a gesture could do nothing but good on both sides.

The year ended sadly for Peter and his mother, for Grandma Ingle died during the Christmas holiday. Since her husband's death in 1939 she had gone on living, proudly independent, in her isolated cottage in the mountains of Wales, until in 1951, the same year as Peter and June were wed, she married an old friend of the family several years her junior, and they lived there happily together for the next fourteen years. Now, at the age of ninety-two, her story had come to a close and, reluctantly, for she had kept her indomitable spirit to the last, but with the will to accept the inevitable, she released her grasp on life and on December 26th slipped quietly away.

Early in February 1966 the film cameras moved into Peter's home. Eric Knowles, chairman of the Double Run Cine Group, had met Peter at Christmas through buying the Association's Christmas cards and, impressed by his cheerful personality, had asked if he might do a film about his life.

Shooting took place in the evenings and weekends throughout February and March. The family were filmed having breakfast at lunchtime. This was hardly their normal time of rising, but as Knowles was an amateur cameraman, it happened to be the only time he had free. So after consuming a more than adequate lunch they then had to start on cereal, toast and coffee for the benefit of the movie camera.

After breakfast the film proceeds to show Peter in his study opening a letter with his toes, which turns out to be a commission for a painting of a moonlight landscape. He then phones his correspondent. But there is no answer, so with his toes he inserts writing paper into the typewriter which is on the floor and types a reply with his half shoe and tapper. With his foot he extracts the letter, folds it, inserts it into an envelope, flips it on to the table, licks the stamp and affixes it with his chin, seals the envelope, picks it up with his mouth and posts it in the letter box outside. We then see Peter painting the picture with the brush held in his mouth, and the film ends with a shot of Peter's correspondent opening her parcel and hanging the completed painting on the wall of her home.

The theme music for the film was composed and played by Len Makinson, and the commentary given by Peter himself. The film, entitled The Second Door, was entered for the National Top Eight Competition, in which it won a Merit Award. Of it the judges said, "Peter Spencer tells his own story on the sound track with an engaging directness. This is a very competently produced and compelling film which presents its subject matter in a straightforward and interesting way. Refreshingly devoid of sentimentality, it puts many more ambitious so-called inspirational films in the shade."

The year 1966 was a sad one for June, for on March 11th her father died. June grieved over his death as she had always been close to him, and Mrs. Linnett was completely overwhelmed by her loss. As the Linnetts had moved to Wallasey following Mr. Linnett's retirement in 1957, June was able to look after her mother when she became ill, for now she lived only ten minutes away.

Mrs. Linnett had, by now, completely changed her opinion of Peter's suitability as a husband for June. Although, temperamentally, they were complete opposites, Mrs. Linnett had a great respect for his character and for what he had achieved.

That Spring Peter was kept very busy canvassing, and in May of that year he was re-elected as Councillor for Marlowe Ward with an increased majority of 645.

In the following month June had a short holiday in Las Palmas to refresh her while Peter stayed at the BLESMA Home in Crieff. This had recently been built at a cost of £75,000, all raised by voluntary subscriptions, and contained all the latest appliances for the disabled, including a Clos-o-Mat automatic toilet. This ingenious apparatus precludes the use of toilet paper, for at the touch of a switch it washes with warm water and dries with warm air. Peter believes this is one of the finest aids ever invented for the disabled and he has one at home. A further development suggested by him, a portable, foot-operated pump model, has now been produced.

The staff at Crieff were very friendly and understanding and while he was there Peter did a painting of the Drummond Arms Pier at St. Fillans, which he presented to the Home.

It was during this month that work was commenced on an extension to Peter and June's small bungalow to provide two extra rooms in the roof. With two active children and the necessity for Peter to have a study where he could teach elocution and deal with his voluminous correspondence, they were threatening to burst out of the bungalow's seams, and it had become essential to have more space.

For six months Peter and June lived in a whirlwind of hammering, painting, "Over to you, Jack", seething dust and the making of countless cups of tea. The children had a field day, zooming in and out of the littered rooms, managing to cover themselves first in paint, then in tar.

"I'm a space man! Yahoo!" Robin leapt off the tenth, bare, newly constructed stair and landed amongst a roll of wallpaper. "I'm searching for a new planet!"

"Me too!" shouted four-year-old Jill, jumping with a plop off the second stair. "I'm a *bigger* space man, and I'm going to beat you!" and with a whoop she tore after Robin into the tiny garden.

It was in the garden that Peter had his studio, an outhouse twelve feet by seven feet, with a wide expanse of window on the north side. Here he retired for peace and quiet in order to paint. The studio was littered with canvases and there was one on the easel awaiting his attention. A painting of the three Wise Men on camels, standing on a ridge overlooking the lights of Bethlehem. It was a Christmas card design on which he was trying to concentrate, but so many things and people encroached upon his time; so many responsibilities and requests for help. "Please would you . . . judge the children's painting competition, present the prizes, give a little talk, become a Vice-President of the local Spastics Association, attend the Recreations Committee and decide who is going to run the boating lake. And don't forget the Libraries Committee tomorrow, the Disablement Advisory Committee on Monday, the Mayor's party for children this afternoon, the Disabled Persons Swimming Club Draw, the Council Meeting, BLESMA Meeting, Caucus Meeting... And will you become Chairman of this and Chairman of that." And always with a smile Peter would acquiesce for he liked being busy, and in spite of it all he managed to turn out a large number of paintings in a year, some for the Association to be used as greetings cards or in the yearly calendar, some for private individuals.

In October Peter went with the Wallasey and District Disabled Persons Swimming Club to Pietra Ligure in Italy. This was quite an experience. There was such a feeling of camaraderie and good fellowship amongst the helpers and the helped, a spirit of joy which was wholly infectious. They were so glad to be alive. They gloried in the sea and the sun and the freedom from confinement, the brief but glorious release from sticks and wheelchairs.

The trip started off quite soberly but turned into a riot of good humoured banter and laughter. The helpers came from all walks of life, some from Rotary Clubs, while others were simply friends who had volunteered. Everyone was called by their Christian name and there was an atmosphere of complete informality from the beginning.

Sixty-three disabled people and their helpers left Liverpool on September 29th, five by car, eight by train and the rest by plane to Genoa. This created quite a stir, as fourteen of the disabled were in wheelchairs which had to be hoisted on to the plane by a fork lift. The chairs were then folded and stacked in the aircraft, which arrived at Genoa airport in an outsize storm to the accompaniment of violent thunder and forked lightning. The members were hoisted off the plane, put back in their wheelchairs and pushed to the coach which was to take them to Pietra Ligure.

By the time they reached the hotel the rain had stopped and the sun was shining. The staff came out to meet them looking slightly shaken. They had never seen anything quite like this before. In addition to the fourteen in wheelchairs, two members were blind, and several were on sticks. In Italy it appeared to be the practice to keep the disabled out of sight, away from the general throb of life. However, they soon became used to their rather unusual guests and were relieved to find they did not create quite the chaos that had been anticipated.

Peter's friend, Charles Cowlin, helped him to bath, dress and shave, and towelled him down after a swim. For the people in wheelchairs a type of rickshaw was devised, carried on poles by four burly helpers. A long strip of matting was placed before them, they walked down this in procession, lowered their charges into the sea and watched them float away as free and as happy as seals.

Peter was asked to arrange the excursions and they went by coach into the mountains; to San Remo with its beautiful yachts and harbour; and to Alassio at night, where they visited a nightclub complete with wheelchairs. Then, well fed, tanned and relaxed, satiated with sun and sea air, they started their journey home. The staff, who were now their friends, all lined up with genuine affection to say farewell. Peter was of the opinion that anyone who had lost faith in human nature might easily revive it by going on holiday with the members of the Disabled Persons Swimming Club.

On the plane Peter joined the pilots in the cockpit as they approached the French coast. Aircraft had greatly changed since the days he had been in Transport Command, but he still gained a thrill from sitting at the controls. These were being operated by George, the automatic pilot, while Peter chatted to the first pilot who, he was interested to discover, had been receiving his training in Oklahoma, U.S.A. at the same time as Peter had been a cadet in Florida.

The flight over England was fascinating. Darkness had descended and the millions of lights of London were glittering like fairyland so that all the landmarks were clearly visible, cast in a golden light. Peter had never seen London like this for, when he had flown during the war, London, like all English cities, had been totally blacked out. It was an exciting contrast and a satisfying climax to his trip.

During October, shortly after his return from holiday, Peter was invited to become a director of a new business venture, a small travel agency in Wallasey which had expanded into a limited company. After some initial difficulty in finding and registering a name which was sufficiently dissimilar to the many others already in use in the travel world, they decided on Transolar Travel Ltd., and at the first meeting Peter was asked to become Chairman. In due course the firm again expanded and a second and larger office was opened at Bebington in Cheshire.

Then followed the second Wallasey Arts Festival. A slightly more ambitious project than the previous one, it included ballet, concerts, opera, art exhibitions and Spanish dancing. In this, its second year, the Festival had really begun to establish itself not only in the hearts and minds of the people of Wallasey but also with many who came from much further afield.

At the end of November, June appeared with the Wallasey Operatic Society as Lalume, a seducer of men, in "Kismet", which was presented at the Royal Court Theatre, Liverpool, in aid of charity. She was wholly enthralled by the show. For six weeks she lived in a rare and exciting world. Because June was the true professional, everything had to be perfect: her costumes, her makeup, her lines, her knowledge and grasp of the character she was portraying.

She had to plan and organise and work doubly hard at home in order to fit the show into her life without disrupting it, but it was worth all the effort involved. The stimulus such an event provided, the enthusiastic reception and applause of the audience were nectar to her.

This was not the life that June had visualised for herself when she first met Peter. She had dreamed of becoming a famous singer and of Peter shining in her reflected glory. But, by one of life's unexpected twists, it was Peter who had won the acclaim, and in the course of time June had accepted that this was the better way.

With her family around her she was content, for she was the hub, the centre of their universe; their world revolved around her. Without her none of it might have been. Her stage appearances gave June the excitement and adulation she needed; her family provided the ballast, the security and love which were a vital, necessary, and irreplaceable part of her life. By her own endeavours she had gained a place in both worlds and she gave herself to both unstintingly.

In 1967 June had a show of her own. With B.B.C. organist Charles Smitton, she appeared at the Floral Pavilion Theatre, New Brighton in "Two's Company", a light hearted family musical entertainment presented by Wallasey Corporation every afternoon from July to September. This was as much fun for June as it was for the audience, with whom she and Charles Smitton built up a special rapport. The audience were completely involved, taking a delighted and active part in the show. Children came up from the auditorium, sang with June and joined in "Party Piece Time" and the various quiz games which were thought up by June and Peter. It resembled a big family party in which everyone enjoyed themselves and joined in, and proved to be so popular that it was repeated in the following year.

At the end of the last show in the season the customary presents were handed over the footlights. A box of chocolates, one or two small packets, some flowers, and then June found herself holding a soft, white, woolly bundle. It was warm! Two bright eyes in a tiny face were looking up at her trustingly. An accompanying card announced that this was Suki, an eight weeks old pedigree toy poodle, a present from an unknown admirer. June, for once, was at a loss for words; but more was to follow when, as further gifts, came a dog basket, a blanket, a collar and lead, a brush and comb, two dishes and a book on how to look after a poodle.

Jill, who was with Peter in the audience, rushed excitedly on to the stage and in a loud voice for all to hear pleaded, "We can keep it, Mummy, can't we? Daddy said we couldn't have a puppy." Peter, feeling more like a wicked uncle, remembered that for months past the children had been saying how much they would like a puppy and how on more than one occasion he had said, "No. Mummy has enough to do."

Now he could not possibly refuse and Suki became a much-loved member of the family. The unknown admirer has continued to remain unknown.

During 1966 Peter gave an illustrated talk to a group of Occupational Therapists in Liverpool. One of the therapists in the audience was particularly interested in the talk and the coloured slides which Peter presented showing what had been achieved by the various artists of the Association. She mentioned to Peter that one of her charges in hospital was sixteen-year-old Stephen Smith who had fractured his neck while diving into shallow water, with the result that all four limbs were paralysed.

She had already introduced Stephen to the art of painting with the brush held in his mouth and he had proved to be a keen and adept pupil.

Peter went to see and talk to Stephen while he was still in hospital and gave him the address of Jimmy Rodolfos, the American artist, who had been injured in the same way, whom he had recently met at the Canadian conference. Just before Stephen left to return home, Peter gave a slide show at the hospital for the benefit of the boy and his parents, which was also watched with close interest by several doctors and some of the other disabled patients.

It was Peter's hope that by demonstrating just how much it was possible to achieve in spite of his paralysis, Stephen would be armed against frustration and despair and the more ready to cope with some of the difficulties which he was bound to encounter in the world outside the hospital walls. Peter's desire to help in this way was deepend by his very keen awareness that there had been no one similarly to inspire him in the early years of his own disablement. He regretted those wasted years.

Stephen turned out to be a gratifyingly gifted pupil at art and had also been learning to type. It gave him much pleasure to be able to send Peter a typewritten letter of appreciation for his interest and help.

Early in 1966 the Association of Mouth and Foot Painters had held an exhibition of paintings in Frankfurt during which all the proceeds from the paintings sold were donated to a special group of disabled children in Germany. These were children who had been born irreparably damaged by the drug contergen, known in England as thalidomide, which had been prescribed to their mothers during pregnancy.

Anxious to extend such a scheme to include others, Peter proposed that a similar exhibition might be held in London to aid the British child victims of the drug. He wrote to Lady Hoare, the chairman of the British

Thalidomide Appeal Trust, and received a letter from Brigadier Chatterton, the Hon. Administrator of the Appeal, to say:

> "Lady Hoare has asked me to thank you for your letter, and both she and I are delighted by your offer to hold an exhibition for this Appeal. We both feel that this would be an excellent idea, and are grateful for your support..."

A few days later the three of them met in Liverpool to discuss the plans for its fruition.

Lady Hoare had first launched her Appeal in 1962 when she and Sir Frederick were Lord and Lady Mayoress of London. The deeper Lady Hoare had gone into the matter the more concerned she had become at its gravity and the fact that no concerted action seemed to have been taken on a national scale. A tenacious and brilliant campaigner for the causes in which she believed, she therefore formed a committee and started to travel throughout Britain and Germany to study the situation at first hand and discover the most effective way of dealing with it.

"As most of these children are without arms or legs, and sometimes both, the main need was for artificial limbs which would give them mobility," she told Peter. "In Heidelberg, Brigadier Chatterton and I were very impressed with the advances being made in gas-powered limbs, and we arranged to import the parts necessary to make them here, particularly the upper limbs in which very little advance had been achieved in England."

Not long after this they travelled to Russia to see the bio-electric arm which had been developed there to obey electric impulses from the brain. The Trust contracted to buy the licence and were sent a prototype of the limb which was paid for by an anonymous donor.

The British public were very generous in their support

and funds were used to bring together and develop all the various sources of help throughout the country, in hospitals, welfare departments and research establishments.

"These children are of normal intelligence," said Lady Hoare. "Their handicap is physical not mental, and it is our aim to help them to lead as normal and active a life as possible."

This was an aim with which Peter could wholeheartedly concur. He was anxious to hold the exhibition of paintings as soon as possible, but he and Brigadier Chatterton experienced considerable difficulty in finding a suitable venue. The Royal Academy and several galleries in the West End of London were approached, but they were all booked for many months ahead. Finally it was decided to hold the exhibition at the Royal Exchange in the City of London.

In order to publicise the exhibition, Lady Hoare held a morning cocktail party at the Press Club to which she invited the artists, the thalidomide parents, and the press. Peter, June and the majority of the English artists were present, and June, with her cheerful and outgoing nature, played happily with the thalidomide children there. Although these children's bodies were malformed their faces were beautiful. They possessed an alert and keen intelligence and were already learning to adjust themselves to the effective use of artificial limbs. Young Tommy Yendell – born without arms – was also sufficiently agile to turn gleeful somersaults across the carpeted floor.

Of the Mouth and Foot Painting Artists, Richard Hext had been driven all the way up from Devon by his brother that morning, Albert Baker had come from the Cheshire Home in Liss, and Heather Strudwick's husband had brought her by ambulance in a wheelchair from Essex.

Peter had met Heather before while she was still living in hospital. She was a friendly young woman with an attractive smile and personality who, though she was

Peter speaking on behalf of the artists at the Lady Hoare Thalidomide Appeal Exhibition of the Mouth & Foot Painting Artists held in the Royal Exchange, London, in April 1967. L to R : Peter H. H. Massey, Lady Hoare, Erich Stegmann, Sir Frederick Hoare

Peter's specially adapted shoe and typewriter. Note the wristwatch worn on the ankle.

Photo by Bob Bird

Peter seated in his specially adapted Mini. *Above*, details of the controls.

Photo by *"Daily Mirror"*

The Spencer family in 1970, complete with Suki.

Photo by Bob Bird

paralysed from the neck down, gave every appearance of enjoying her life. But this had not always been so.

Heather contracted polio at the age of twenty-four. A few months later she lost the two people most dear to her, first her husband who left her to seek solace elsewhere, and whom she eventually divorced; then her baby son, Paul, who was adopted by her sister-in-law. Agreeing to his adoption was an agonising decision for Heather, but she knew it was in his best interests. Then she lost her unborn child.

"I don't know how I survived that period," she told Peter. "I think the turning point came when I was first taught to frog breathe, a method of pumping air through the mouth with the tongue and sending it straight down into the lungs. It gave me some form of independence, as it meant I wasn't now *wholly* dependent on machines; and I began to fight back.

"First I went on a visit in my wheelchair to see my father, an Army Colonel in Brussels, then I learnt to type with a mouthstick. I helped edit a magazine called *Puffin* and started to write a book. Then, a decision which was to have a very important effect on my life: I began to paint and was eventually admitted to the Association as a student member. After this I paid a visit to my sister in America, travelling on the *Queen Elizabeth* with a special portable bed."

"A positive whirlwind of activity," said Peter.

"Yes! Wasn't it?" Heather's blue eyes smiled at him. "Then came the most important decision of all. I was moved to another hospital and met Ronald Strudwick who was working as a porter there. We fell in love and were married in September 1966, and now we have our own bungalow. We are so happy there. You don't know how wonderful it is to have a place of one's own after all those years!"

"I think I do," said Peter quietly.

The Exhibition in Aid of Thalidomide Children was officially opened by Sir Frederick Hoare on April 24th, 1967. In his opening speech he said:

"You will see here over a hundred and forty paintings from thirty different countries. This is a truly international exhibition. Some may consider it to be a sad occasion. I do not agree with them. I think it is most remarkable to see pictures painted by people with such handicaps but such human sympathy of thought that they have decided to hold this exhibition in order to help children with similar disabilities. You may have seen Mickie May, one of the thalidomide children, at the door to greet me. I believe it is true to say that these children are above average in the beauty of expression of their faces, and in their intelligence. As one of the Trustees of the Fund I see them getting older each day and you can imagine the extent to which the difficulties of their lives become greater, but the sympathy and generosity of the public has done a tremendous amount to help these children."

This was followed by a few words from Erich Stegmann and Peter, and then three paintings, by Stegmann, Peter and Elizabeth Twistington-Higgins, were put up for auction and realised nearly a hundred guineas. Peter's painting was of the *Empress of Canada* tied up at Liverpool landing stage, and was bought by Canadian Pacific.

Peter was glad of the chance to have a chat with several of the artists at the exhibition, particularly Elizabeth Twistington-Higgins, as although they had corresponded and he had written to welcome her when she was first accepted by the Association, they had not previously met.

Elizabeth had been a ballet dancer; dancing was her life. But in 1953 she was struck down by polio and life as she had known it was over. Then followed months of black despair, for she was paralysed from the neck down and lived for over two years in an iron lung. But she had many friends both in the hospital and outside it; one of them introduced her to painting and this proved the release she had been searching for. Here with her paintbrush she could bring to life all that she had lost. She could re-create all the joy and fluid movement of the ballet. Her graceful paintings were reproduced by Medici and also used on menu cards, several of which Peter had seen when travelling on the Cunard Line. She joined the Association and devoted herself to art, turning out an astonishing number of paintings every month, sitting in her wheelchair and painting with the brush in her mouth at an electrically operated easel. As she has limited movement in her head, this enables the canvas to be moved in different directions so that she can produce larger paintings. With the renewed confidence which her success had given her, she decided to go on a cruise and was given V.I.P. treatment in Israel, Egypt and Morocco.

"Then," she told Peter, a smile lighting up her thin face, "I was able to buy a small but charming flat near Deal overlooking the sea and pay for someone to look after me during the day. I have to go back to hospital at night, but it is so wonderful to have my freedom during the day after all those long years of hospital regulations and routine."*

John Chapman, another English artist at the exhibition, was an old friend of Peter's for they had corresponded and met on several occasions. He had been born with curvature of the spine and without arms. From an early age Chapman had learnt to do everything with his feet. He and his wife used to drive about the countryside on a tandem bicycle. He was also a crack shot, holding the gun to his shoulder with his foot and pulling the trigger with his toe. He had three children. In his early days

---

* Elizabeth Twistington-Higgins has since written her autobiography, appropriately entitled *Still Life*.

he had known poverty, but now thanks to the Association he was able to support his family in reasonable comfort, and was delighted that for the first time in his life he was earning enough to pay income tax!

"I've now got a car," he told Peter, "and it's specially adapted so that I can drive with my feet, using my toes as fingers. It's only a one seater but it's a great help being able to get about on my own."

The idea of one day being able to drive a car had been in Peter's mind for some time and in 1968, while chatting to Geoffrey Harding, Wallasey's Passenger Transport Manager, he mentioned, almost casually, that he thought it would be possible to convert the new automatic Mini to foot controls. Geoffrey Harding, already an inventor of considerable repute with his ingenious adaptations of the hovercraft principle, immediately regarded this suggestion as an interesting and worthwhile challenge and he set to work.

The steering wheel and column were replaced by a disc at foot level, operated by the left foot. The positions of the brake and accelerator pedals were moved, the hand brake became a "heel" brake and the position of the automatic gear selection control was moved to be operated by the right heel. All other switches, such as the ignition/starter, the choke, lights, indicators and windscreen wipers were moved to be in easy reach of the right foot. A handle was fitted at foot level to open and close the door.

It looked bizarre, but it all worked and Geoffrey Harding drove it over a thousand miles in exhaustive tests on long runs, on the skid pan and in all weather conditions.

On May 13th, 1969, with the co-operation of the Department of Social Security and the approval of the Ministry of Transport, the little blue car without a steering wheel was taken on the open road by Peter, accompanied by an instructor from the British School of Motoring. Had anything untoward happened, there was

182

nothing the instructor could have done. Except, as Peter said, for him to jump out . . .

On one occasion, thinking his pupil was driving rather near to a parked car, the instructor instinctively grabbed at where the steering wheel should have been – and found nothing!

"I'm afraid you'll just have to rely on me," Peter reassured him.

They both derived considerable amusement from the startled expressions of other motorists when they saw a car apparently steering itself.

Although the horse-power of the Mini's engine was nothing like that of the aircraft he had once flown, Peter found it a great thrill to have a machine under his control again. He had never driven a car before, but two months later he took the driving test and was delighted when the examiner signed and presented him with the pink slip which meant he had passed first time.

Another milestone in the struggle for independence had been reached. No longer did Peter have to rely on the kindness of his friends: now he could offer *them* lifts. He could come and go as he pleased, transport his paintings, take the family out and enjoy the use of a car as any other motorist does.

A journey which gave him particular satisfaction came three weeks after passing his test, when he drove to Manchester to demonstrate the car. An official of the Automobile Association had telephoned a few days earlier to ask if he could help a young lady, Janet Haley, who lived in Doncaster. As a result of polio, she was unable to use her arms but, having heard of Peter's success, she felt it might be possible for her to drive a foot-operated Mini. Meeting in Manchester, she was impressed with the way Peter was able to handle (or, as he says, "footle") the car; and an interested automobile engineer who had accompanied her from Doncaster made notes of Geoffrey Harding's conversion with a view to similarly adapting a Mini.

Less than six months later, Peter was delighted to hear from Janet that a car had been converted for her and that she, too, had passed her driving test.

Peter knew exactly how she felt.

Chapter Fifteen

ONE OF the Association's exhibitions organised by Peter
was held at the Magee Galleries in Belfast and in May he
flew to attend the opening.

This was to be an occasion of memories, for Peter was
introduced to two "old friends" whom he had never previously met. One was Mrs. Kay Erskine, who had been a
night sister when Peter was at the R.A.F. Hospital in
Halton.

"Peter was in hospital quite a while, but he never knew
me," she told the *Belfast News Letter*, who reported the
event. "I was one of the many nurses who looked after
him. When I heard that he was coming to Belfast I felt
I had to have a word with him. I had known for some
while that he was one of the painters who belonged to the
Association as I had seen his name on several of the
Christmas cards."

After the Exhibition Dr. and Mrs. Erskine met Peter
and June for a drink and a chat, and were most interested to hear about his activities since those sorrowful
days after his accident.

"Remembering you then, lying on that hospital bed
completely helpless, it seems almost unbelievable that
your horizons could have widened so much," said Mrs.
Erskine.

The other "old friend" was the enormous Belfast
Freighter, his painting of which was among those on dis-

play at the Exhibition. He had painted it from photographs, but when he actually saw the plane it was so large that he felt walking around inside it was rather like being swallowed up by the Mersey Tunnel.

Then followed a series of exhibitions in aid of the Thalidomide Appeal. In January 1968 an exhibition was held at the McLellan Galleries in Glasgow which was opened by the Lord Provost. This show was given a detailed commentary by the Art Critic of the *Glasgow Herald*, who headed his article:

IMPRESSIVE EXHIBITION BY MOUTH AND FOOT ARTISTS
This is an exhibition of ninety paintings in which the general standard is such that it outclasses many an exhibition seen recently in this gallery. The exhibits range from abstract designs to paintings of photographic detail ... Of the several excellent still lifes Manuel Parreno's is perhaps the most surprising. It is a large composition of bottles and fruit. Hardly less remarkable, and certainly no less technically assured, is Peter Spencer's Still Life with Books.

In the abstract field six paintings by Marie Louise Tovae are outstanding, while in The Bridge by Moreno Toledo the effect is Van Gogh-like ... Pieter Moleveld's pleasant landscape, Windmills, has a powerful sense of movement, and some of the smaller exhibits are charming, notably E. Twistington-Higgin's Children's Derby.

In some paintings the technique has outstripped artistic perception but on the whole this is a very worthwhile exhibition by any standards.

The paintings are all for sale, ranging from six to fifty guineas. There is also an exhibition of pictures done by thalidomide children. The Association of Mouth and Foot Painters are to award prizes and will encourage the children to become apprenticed to the Association.

In February an exhibition was held in Edinburgh and the B.B.C. Scottish Television News filmed Peter at work. The next day a photo of Peter painting appeared in the *Daily Record* with Lady Hoare's daughter Marinella posing as his model.

The following May, Peter arranged an exhibition at Lewis's store in Liverpool. The exhibition was opened by the Lord Mayor and the store erected a fountain into which the public might throw coins in aid of the thalidomide children. This show was one of the best attended and most financially successful, largely due to the warmhearted co-operation of the store concerned. So much so that, not long after, Peter made arrangements to hold a similar exhibition at Selfridges store in London. Altogether the Association was able to raise a considerable sum for this cause which it has so much at heart.

During the previous October Peter had attended a particularly nostalgic reunion. One hundred R.A.F. British Flying Training School ex-cadets, all of whom had received their training at Clewiston, Florida, during the war, were reunited at the Royal Aero Club in London. Here Peter met once again the friends of his youth, some of whom he had not seen for over twenty years.

Of his three special buddies only Peter Orchard and Monty Manners were there. Peter Pullen, always the keenest of them all, had remained in the R.A.F. and was now a Squadron Leader in Transport Command, stationed with R.A.F. Gatow in Berlin. The reunion had been arranged by Tony Linfield who had been at Clewiston on Course 18. It was a meeting full of reminiscences. As Peter chatted with friends from the past, snatches of conversation drifted towards him: "Do you remember old...?" "So I throttled back and..." "I think it was in Miami when . . ." "I wouldn't have recognised you . . ." recalling memories of golden days in the sun, of comradeship and laughter. And so much in between. Remembering the thrill of receiving his Wings – and then – Transport Command – the Rhine Crossing – and that never to be forgotten day of terror and anguish – March 27th, 1945: the almost empty airfield, the sudden sickening crash, followed by instant oblivion . . .

It all came flooding back to him – the dream which had turned into a nightmare – the seemingly endless years spent in hospitals and rehabilitation centres – the long haul back, painfully climbing out of the pit of pain and despair – back to battle with the world again, and his own physical inadequacy. A world now at "peace", if such a word could be used without irony. But a world which, for Peter, would never be the same again – in which he, irreparably handicapped, must find a place.

"And what do you *want* to do Peter?" Squadron Leader O'Beirne looking at him with kindly, puzzled eyes.

Reading O'Beirne's thoughts: "What part can a man play in society when he is without arms?"

"I would like to become a useful member of the community again . . ."

The false starts, his discharge from the Air Force for "ceasing to fulfil physical requirements", his tentative attempts at completing his own rehabilitation, at winning acceptance in the world at large. The doubts and fears – would it ever be possible to find a niche, not to be pushed into some backwater?

He did not want pity, he wanted independence, and he had fought to achieve it, and to help others to gain it with him. Once he refused to let bitterness overcome him he found there was much kindness in the world, that people were prepared to help him, so long as he helped himself. If they saw him struggling to achieve something, most of them would lend a helping hand.

Disability is such a waste of time. There is the frustration of not being able to do the small physical acts swiftly and smoothly, of never being able to bath or dress oneself. All these things he has accepted, schooling himself to have patience both with himself and with others, and on a normal day he can cope with it all. It is when he has had a restless night that the difficulties threaten to overcome him: nights when the pain is bad and he tosses and turns unable to sleep. The following day his shoulders ache and the nerve pain in both "hands" and the phantom arm is so intense that he does not know what to do with himself and everything takes longer and seems more difficult to do. Yet always he must endeavour to conceal it.

Life is not and can never again be easy. It is the little things he misses, those which others take for granted. He rarely allows himself to look back, but nothing can ever quite compensate for the fact that he will never again play the piano, never put his arms around his wife, ruffle the hair of his children, pick up a fine glass and feel its satisfying smoothness, touch with his hands the velvety softness of a rose, the undulating pattern of a stone found on the beach, or the rough harshness of tweed. Never again be able to pick a book from the shelf and browse through its pages.

But Peter has always counted his blessings, and these are many: his wife and children (Robin has already set his heart on becoming a pilot, and shows a keen interest in all sport, while Jill has taken to the piano and ballet as a baby bird does to the air); his parents, without whose selfless devotion he might not now be here; his many good friends; his acceptance by society; his success as an artist; and his total involvement in the community. If he permits himself to glance back to the days of dark despair in the 1940's, it seems almost unbelievable that life could have changed so much, or brought such fulfilment.

His successes he has laid at June's feet. In the words of the song he wrote for her:

> This is my heart, so faithful and true,
> This is my love just for you.

What lies ahead for Peter Spencer? Every day is a challenge, and he has accepted that challenge aware of all that it entails.

I cannot do better than close this book with the words of a song which Peter wrote inspired by its title:

> No man an island
> No man can be
> Without another
> To set him free
> To taste the good things
> To shun the bad
> To love and be loved
> No heart is sad.
>
> No man an island
> No man is born
> Without a reason
> To greet each dawn
> To face the future
> With hopes and fears
> No time for crying
> No time for tears . . .

Epilogue
by
Peter Spencer

To SAY that I hope you have enjoyed this book would not be quite true. Parts of it are definitely not enjoyable, but I do hope that what you have read has been of interest and has perhaps given you a little food for thought.

When Eileen Waugh asked if she might write this biography, I agreed; not because I imagined myself to be a handsome hero or that you would say, "What a story!" when you finally put the book down, but because I felt that whatever came out in the writing might do some good to someone somewhere.

There are still people who have accidents and lose limbs, and for these people – once they have adjusted themselves mentally and accepted the disability – there will be gadgets, devices and helpful inventions which will become part of their everyday lives. The gadgets mentioned in the previous pages (e.g. the plastic mouthpiece for painting, the "finger" on my foot for typing and the telephone device) are simple and have been made locally. Other inventions, such as the converted car and the automatic toilet, are more complicated and consequently more expensive.

Of course, many things still elude and frustrate me and some things must be totally disregarded. But should you feel that I could give any useful advice or encouragement to others, please feel free to contact me (through the publishers and I will do all I can. On page 189 is the sentence "Disability is such a waste of time". This is very true and makes the phrase "Get cracking!" (which my wife often uses to me!) even more so.

If the reading of NO MAN AN ISLAND results in helping just one disabled person to "get cracking" sooner than he or she might have done, then its publication will have been justified.

Wallasey, 1970   PETER SPENCER

Index